CHRISTMAS PROGRAMS for the CHURCH

compiled by
PAT FITTRO

STANDARD PUBLISHING

Cincinnati, Ohio

Standard Publishing, Cincinnati, Ohio
A division of Standex International Corporation
© 2000 by Standard Publishing

ISBN 0-7847-1168-2

Contents

Christmas Springs From Love

Lillian Robbins

Characters:
WOMAN
MOM
DAD (Frank)
RANDY, a twelve-year-old boy
NARRATOR
MARY
JOSEPH
INNKEEPER
SHEPHERDS (number optional)
WISE MEN (number optional)
SINGERS (either soloist or group)

Act I
   Scene 1—In the world
   Scene 2—In a home before Christmas
   Scene 3—In the home on Christmas morning

Act II—A pageant at the church
   Scene 1—The inn of Bethlehem
   Scene 2—The stable

Props: two chairs, small table, lamp, magazine and newspaper, magazine rack, decorated Christmas tree, manger, baby doll, stool, shepherd's crooks, gifts for wise men, spotlight, tape of a crying baby

Costumes: contemporary clothing for family; long cloaks, headdress for biblical characters

Act I—Scene 1

In the world. Lights out for a few minutes before beginning the play. Curtains open. Stage is lighted just enough for audience to see Woman and to

*notice her appearance. She is barefoot, dressed in ragged clothes, has di-
sheveled hair. She is hysterical, flinging her arms, running around stage,
looking around and up toward the ceiling.*

WOMAN: Help! Help! Help! I'm lost! I'm lost! Somebody help me.
   Somebody help me!

*(There is a brief pause in her screaming, and the voice of a crying baby can
be heard. The woman gradually becomes calm and settles down prostrate on
the floor. The baby's crying stops. Slowly the curtain closes.)*

Scene 2

*In a home a few weeks before Christmas. Mom is reading a magazine and
Dad is reading a newspaper.*

MOM: I don't know what in the world we can give Randy for Christ-
   mas this year. You know we've already given him everything.
DAD: Right.
MOM: I just don't know what else we can get for him.
DAD *(not paying any attention):* Uh-huh.
MOM: Even when he was a little tot, he got every toy he ever asked
   for. You remember when he was three that we got him a bike that
   was way too big for the little fellow?
DAD: Uh-huh.
MOM: Frank, you're not listening to me again.
DAD *(lowers his paper):* What did you say, Dear?
MOM: I was talking about Christmas—and Randy. I just don't know
   anything left to give him. *(Dad begins to read again.)* He's only
   twelve years old, but he has everything. Frank, I wish you would
   listen to me!
DAD *(looks up again):* Sure, Dear, what was it about Randy?
MOM: It's about Christmas. We are already into November and we
   haven't made any plans for Randy's Christmas for this year.
DAD: What do you want to do?
MOM: First of all, I want you to think about it. It's been on my mind
   for weeks. So, what can we do? What can we give him?
DAD: Oh, I don't know. Give him a TV for his room.
MOM: Frank, you know we gave him a color TV last year.

DAD: Oh, yeah, I forgot. Well, how about a stereo?

MOM: He just got a new one for his birthday. And you know what bothers me? He never seems to really appreciate anything. He just takes everything for granted, like he is just supposed to get everything he wants.

DAD: Well, what do you suggest?

MOM: I was just reading an article in this magazine. It suggests that parents might surprise an ungrateful child by giving him nothing.

DAD: You know we can't do that.

MOM: Well then, you think of something.

DAD: Randy would really be disappointed if he didn't get something really nice.

MOM: I was just thinking, would it make him hostile toward us or maybe help him see how things really are? You know we could try it, and then maybe give him something later.

DAD (goes back to reading): You just make the plans, Dear, and I'll go along with it.

MOM: You always say that, and sometimes I like it that way. But, Frank, I need some help in deciding what is best for Randy. You know at this age he is very impressionable. I don't want to make the wrong decision.

DAD: You'll make a good decision, Dear. I trust you with that.

MOM: All of us may be surprised. We'll just see how it goes.

Scene 3

Christmas morning in the family's house. A tree is decorated, but there are no presents. Mom is just moving around, placing items on table or magazines by the chair. Dad is reading.

RANDY (enters rubbing his eyes): Is it time to get up yet?

MOM: Come on in, Son. It is Christmas morning and it is going to be a beautiful day.

DAD (puts paper down): Good morning, Randy.

RANDY (looking around): Did I get up too early?

MOM: No, we are just having a different Christmas this year. You don't see any presents because Dad and I decided that you already have everything you want. This Christmas we just have this for you. (Goes to Randy and gives him a hug.) We just give you our love, Son, just barrels and barrels of love!

DAD (*coming over and gently pushing Mom aside and hugging Randy*): And from your dad, too, Randy, more love than you can ever know. There is not a box or bag or any kind of wrapper big enough to hold the love I have for you.

RANDY (*holding his dad tight*): Dad, that's really all I ever wanted, just for you to love me. (*Releases Dad.*) Sometimes you are so busy with everything else, I don't know whether you love me or not.

DAD: Of course I love you. I didn't realize you felt that way, Randy.

RANDY: If you could just come to my games sometimes, I would know everything else is not more important to you than I am.

DAD: Oh, Randy, nothing is more important than you. I'm really sorry, Son. We're going to spend a lot more time together from now on.

RANDY: Mom, you know what I'd really like to do? Let's go to that little church around the corner. They are presenting a Christmas pageant this evening.

MOM: That will be wonderful. I haven't seen a Christmas pageant in years. In the meantime, let's go to the kitchen. I have everything ready to prepare a special breakfast. We'll all share it together. Nobody racing off to school or to work. It will just be our time.

(*With Mom's arm and Dad's arm around Randy, they all leave.*)

Act II—Scene 1

At the church. Manger scene, without baby, is placed on far side of the stage. Spotlight is on door to inn on opposite end of stage.

NARRATOR: The time had come for Joseph to go to Bethlehem because of Caesar Augustus' decree that all residents of Israel should return to the city of their ancestors to be taxed. This trip from Nazareth was at an inconvenient time for Joseph and Mary. The journey was long. Mary became very tired. Finally they arrived at the door of the inn in the City of David. Many other travelers had come to this same place seeking shelter for the night.

(*Mary and Joseph enter.*)

JOSEPH (*knocks on door, innkeeper opens door*): We need a place to stay tonight.

Christmas Springs From Love   7

INNKEEPER: I'm sorry. There is no space available in this inn.

JOSEPH: We aren't asking for any special place, just some place where my wife can lie down.

INNKEEPER: There are so many people traveling to Bethlehem. All the rooms are full.

JOSEPH: But surely you have some place for my wife. I can get along anywhere.

INNKEEPER: I wish you had arrived earlier. I just rented my last space to some other men.

JOSEPH: Is there another inn where I could get a room?

INNKEEPER: I'm afraid not.

(Mary shows signs of discomfort, holding on to Joseph, groaning a little.)

JOSEPH: Surely you can help me. Don't you see my wife is expecting a child? This is her first child. The journey has been long, all the way from Nazareth. She must have some rest.

INNKEEPER: You may not even want to hear my suggestion, but it is the only solution to your problem that I can think of.

JOSEPH: Anything, just tell me.

INNKEEPER: There is a stable down the hill. New straw has just been put there. Perhaps you could make a bed of straw for your wife.

JOSEPH *(looks away):* Thank you. You say it's just down the hill? We'll go there. *(Helps Mary as they walk away.)* It will be all right, Mary. At least it will be a place for you to rest.

NARRATOR: Mary and Joseph would have to accept the accommodations offered to them. There was no other way.

Scene 2

The stable. Spotlight is on Mary as she sits beside the manger where the baby lies. Joseph stands.

JOSEPH: Praise God from whom all blessings flow! I knew He would find a way for us. Now your baby is born, Mary, and you are all right. I thank the Lord for this animal's stall. Just look at the precious child lying there. And His name is Jesus.

NARRATOR: In that lonely stable, Mary gave birth to the Son of God. Baby Jesus was laid in a manger. Perhaps Mary and Joseph never expected such a lowly birth, but God had His purpose for such a humble advent for His Son.

Christmas Springs From Love

SINGERS: "Silent Night! Holy Night!"

NARRATOR: On the hillside of Bethlehem, shepherds watched their flock by night. They could talk of the day's events, the encounters with wild animals, or the best place they found water, or a sheep that went astray.

In the stillness of the night, suddenly an angel appeared to them. It was a glorious moment, but the shepherds were afraid. To calm their fears, the angel spoke, "Don't be afraid. I have come to tell you the good news. In the City of David, which is Bethlehem, you will find a baby wrapped in swaddling clothes and lying in a manger. This baby is Christ the Lord."

The shepherds were amazed as a group of angels more than they could number appeared before them and began to praise God and speak of glory to God and peace on earth.

Such glorious, amazing, wonderful news came to those shepherds that night. Their hearts were stirred. "Let's go and see this thing which has come to pass," they said one to another. Across the hills they went to Bethlehem to see for themselves so their eyes could behold Jesus, the promised Messiah.

(Shepherds come forth, look at the baby and kneel.)

SINGERS: "What Child Is This?"

NARRATOR: Sometime later, wise men from the East came to worship the newborn King. Although they didn't understand the full significance of the birth of Jesus, they had been led by a star to where the young child was.

Apparently they were men of wealth who could travel across the land by camel to search for the special child. The men arrived from the East bringing treasures as they came.

(Wise men come forth, present their gifts and kneel.)

NARRATOR: Entering into the presence of Jesus, they laid before Him their gifts of gold, frankincense, and myrrh. The wise men fell down and worshiped the Christ child.

SINGERS: "O Holy Night" *(Be sure to include the second verse.)*

NARRATOR: As I view the nativity, I am reminded of the baby's cry from the first scene in our presentation tonight and of the distraught, lost woman who was so frantically seeking help. As the cry of the infant was heard, the woman found a sense of peace.

And so it is with the coming of Jesus Christ the Savior to a lost world. God had sent His prophets to the people of Bible times. The people had rejected God's messengers, had stoned them, had killed them. Now His only begotten Son would do what never had been done before. This little baby would grow up and provide the people with the promise of salvation for eternity with Him. Individuals need not be lost anymore.

The woman could find no peace and material gifts could not satisfy the young boy because something was missing in their lives. It is love that makes the difference. That's what Christmas is—a glorious demonstration of the love of God as He delivers His Son to the world.

All of Christmas springs from the love of God. Our desire to be joyful, to give to others, to tell the story of Jesus, to worship the Father God and His Christ, to gather our families and friends, to brighten the environment about us with lights and greenery, all these things spring from love. If they do not, then we have missed the meaning of Christmas.

As we mentally witness the scene in the stable of Bethlehem and gaze at the baby Jesus, our hearts are filled with love at so great a gift, and our eyes are opened to the wonderful blessings of God. Oh, what a marvelous Savior!

Will you all stand with me now and join in singing "Joy to the World!" *(Close with prayer.)*

Stuck in a Box

Len Cuthbert

Cast:
DRAYTON, boy, young teen, acts cool and tough, spoiled
STRAT, boy, young teen, friend of Drayton
BLYTH, girl, young teen, upper class
MINDY, girl, young teen, friend of Blyth, plain, quiet
LEWIS, boy, young teen, small
MINDY'S MOM, no dialogue, appears in Mindy Scene only
SINGER, sings in Mindy Scene only

Setting: Main stage is set at stage left as the inside of a large
elevator. This may be created by a single backdrop with a movable
elevator door in the center. The shape of the elevator box may be
created using one or more of the following suggestions:
  • lights that mark off a square on the floor.
  • an overhanging ceiling grid *(lights may shine through)*
  • an elevated floor the shape of the inside of the elevator *(risers)*
Scenes surrounding center stage
Mindy Scene: Downstage center, two chairs (pew style) facing a
  small riser
Blyth Scene: A white eight-foot square, upstage right as a backdrop
Strat Scene: Downstage right: a bedroom door, a window, both self-
  supported. Apart from these is a stack of wrapped gifts. The white
  backdrop in Blyth Scene can be used also.
Church lobby scene

Suggested Music: All songs used as background music only, except
  "I Heard the Bells on Christmas Day" which is sung. You may sub-
  stitute any songs with your own selections.
  "Linus and Lucy," by Vince Guaraldi, from *A Charlie Brown Christmas*
  "I Heard the Bells on Christmas Day," by Henry W. Longfellow
  "You Gotta Get Up," by Rich Mullins, Copyright 1993 Edward
  Grant, Inc. Printed music available in *Rich Mullins, A Liturgy, a
  Legacy and a Ragamuffin Band,* Copyright 1994 Word Music.
  Vocal/solo songbook #301 0269 498 published by Word Music.
  Recording available on Reunion cassette #7010087520 or compact
  disc #7010087725.

Performance Time: About thirty minutes

Time: Late afternoon, Christmas Eve, stores are closing.

At Rise: The inside of an elevator. Door is upstage center. The number indicators change and stop at floor 6. (This is optional. Simple electrical switches with low-voltage bulbs can be operated from behind the set by the same person moving the elevator door.) Upbeat Christmas music opens the scene, possibly "Linus and Lucy" by Vince Guaraldi. The door opens and Drayton and Strat run in racing each other to the control panel.

STRAT *(both are pushing at each other to get at the panel):* Let me push it this time.
DRAYTON: I'm the oldest, I'll do it.
STRAT: Only by sixteen days.
DRAYTON: Nice going, Strat. *(Several floors have been pushed and are lit up.)* Now we're gonna stop at all the floors.
STRAT: Wasn't me. You did it.

(The door begins to close and they both move toward the outside walls facing each other.)

DRAYTON: Me and my brother saw the movie, *Zeroids From Neptune,* last night. It was cool.
STRAT: That's a weird movie. I can't believe your mom let you see it.
DRAYTON: She didn't. She thought we went to see the kid's film. *(Sarcastically.)* Yeah, right! *(The elevator stops at the next floor and the door opens. Just before closing, Drayton jumps out and yells.)* Zeroids attacking! *(He quickly jumps back in.)* C'mon, c'mon, close. *(As the door closes, they both laugh.)*
STRAT: I think I know what I'm getting for Christmas.
DRAYTON: So what! I've already seen my presents and played with some of them.
STRAT: Your mom gave you your gifts already?
DRAYTON: No. I just found them and tested them out.
STRAT: Oh. *(Pause. The door opens and closes at another floor. Excited.)* Hey, Drayton, you want to come to my house when we get home?

DRAYTON: Can't. I have to go out tonight. But maybe I can after I get back.

STRAT: Hey! We could go to your house if you want.

DRAYTON: Nah. My sister has her friend Brenda at our house. All they do is yap, yap, yap and giggle at each other. *(Imitates the giggle.)*

(The elevator has stopped at the third floor and the door opens. As it opens, Blyth and Mindy are there facing each other, giggling, similar to how Drayton imitated. Drayton and Strat look at each other, rolling their eyes.)

BLYTH *(carrying several large packages she has purchased, is swooning as she talks to Mindy)*: He was so-o-o cute.

(Blyth and Mindy realize the elevator door has opened and the boys are staring at them. They enter. They all stare at the numbers above the door as the elevator moves to the next floor. The door opens again at the next floor. Lewis stands waiting to come in.)

LEWIS: Oops. I guess it's pretty full. I'll wait for the next one.

DRAYTON *(leans over to push the "Door Close" button)*: Good. Good-bye!

BLYTH *(steps in the way of the closing door and stops it)*: No. We'll make room. Come on in.

DRAYTON: Hey, wait. It's too crowded and it'll probably be too heavy.

BLYTH *(pointing to the sign)*: The sign says, "Maximum Eight." I count five people . . . that is, if you count yourself as a person.

MINDY *(shy and quietly)*: Blyth.

BLYTH *(to Mindy)*: Mindy, the mall is closing. *(To Lewis.)* You don't want to be stuck here all night, do you? *(Lewis shakes his head.)* Then get in here.

DRAYTON *(to Strat, sarcastically)*: Yeah, right. Like they'd lock you in the mall all night. The guard dogs would eat you first. *(Laughs.)*

LEWIS *(to Blyth, hesitantly)*: Uhhm. Okay. *(He enters the elevator and the door closes behind him. He moves toward the center.)*

BLYTH: I'm Blyth and this is Mindy . . . and just ignore him. *(Gestures toward Drayton.)*

LEWIS: I'm Lewis.

DRAYTON *(pushing Lewis back towards the door)*: You can stand over there, kid.

(As Lewis's back hits the control panel the lights flicker, indicating the elevator stopping.)

Stuck in a Box

MINDY: What was that?

BLYTH: What just happened?

LEWIS: It sounded like we've stopped.

DRAYTON (to Lewis): What did you do?

LEWIS: Nothing! I was just standing here.

DRAYTON (to Blyth): I told you there were too many on this thing. (He starts banging the buttons.)

BLYTH (she grabs Drayton's arm): Stop it. You're going to break it.

STRAT: I think it already is broken.

MINDY: I think I'm feeling faintish.

BLYTH: This is no time for that, Mindy.

LEWIS: It might just be a momentary delay.

DRAYTON: Right, kid.

BLYTH (to Drayton): His name is Lewis.

MINDY: Maybe they've shut all the power off in the mall.

DRAYTON (harshly to Mindy): Now why would they do that?

BLYTH: Leave her alone. Besides, maybe she's right. It is closing time.

STRAT: No, I don't think they would do that.

LEWIS: Yeah. They never shut the elevator power off at night.

MINDY: But . . . it is Christmas Eve.

ALL (look at each other in desperation): Help! (They all push towards the door, sandwiching Lewis.)

LEWIS: Hold it, hold it! I've got it. (They all stop and look at him.) All we have to do is just push the emergency button. It rings the bell and we'll be rescued.

BLYTH: Great idea!

DRAYTON: I was gonna say that.

(Lewis pushes the button, but nothing happens as they all listen quietly.)

MINDY: Sure is a quiet emergency bell.

LEWIS: It must not work.

DRAYTON: Oh, great! (Sarcastically.) Nice idea, kid.

LEWIS: Well, when plan A fails, you try plan B.

MINDY: What's plan B?

LEWIS: Try the emergency phone.

(Strat grabs the emergency phone.)

DRAYTON: I was just thinking that.

BLYTH (sarcastically): You're so clever.

STRAT (into the phone): Hello? Hello. (Taps it and listens again.) It's dead.

14

DRAYTON (*grabs the phone from Strat*): Give me that thing, Strat. (*Into the phone.*) Hey, somebody better get us out of here before w . . . (*Stops and listens.*) It's dead.

LEWIS (*to Strat*): Didn't you already say that?

MINDY (*to Lewis*): I think he already said that.

DRAYTON (*cleverly*): Well, when plan B fails, you try plan C.

BLYTH (*to Drayton*): What's plan C?

DRAYTON (*to Lewis*): Uhmm, what's plan C, kid?

LEWIS: My name is Lewis.

DRAYTON: Okay, Lewis. What's plan C?

LEWIS: I don't know.

MINDY: You don't have a plan C?

BLYTH: Please say you have a plan C.

LEWIS: I don't have a plan C.

DRAYTON (*edgy*): What do you mean, you don't have a plan C? You've got to have another plan, Louie.

LEWIS: Lewis!

STRAT: Hey. Don't be so rough on him, Dray.

BLYTH: Yeah. He came up with two ideas already.

DRAYTON: Hey. Why's everybody attacking me? (*Everyone becomes quietly frustrated. Drayton sits down on the floor.*) Now I'm going to be late . . . and I'll probably end up missing Christmas.

STRAT: What do you care? You've already seen your presents.

MINDY: You've seen your presents?

BLYTH: Probably already broke them too.

DRAYTON (*to Blyth*): Just one.

STRAT: I know! Maybe if we make enough noise, someone will hear us.

MINDY: Hey, let's sing Christmas carols!

DRAYTON: We're stuck in an elevator on Christmas Eve and she wants to sing Christmas carols.

LEWIS: What else would you want to sing on Christmas Eve?

DRAYTON: Let's not sing at all. How about that, Louie?

LEWIS (*to Drayton*): Lewis! Lewis! It's not that difficult!

DRAYTON (*backing off*): Okay, okay.

MINDY (*pause*): How about "I Heard the Bells on Christmas Day"?

DRAYTON: You've got to be kidding. What kind of song is that?

BLYTH: I don't think I've ever heard it.

MINDY: It's my favorite.

LEWIS: What about "Jingle Bells" or "Here Comes Santa Claus" or how about "Frosty the Snowman"?

DRAYTON: Those are kid's songs.

LEWIS (to Drayton): Yeah? Well I am a kid.

MINDY: "I Heard the Bells on Christmas Day" brings back great memories. I first heard it at a Christmas Eve church service.

BLYTH: I didn't know you went to church.

MINDY: Sometimes. I go every year on Christmas Eve—with my mom. (Pause. Disappointed.) Except this year. I was supposed to meet her at the church tonight. (Checks her watch.) She's going to be so worried.

STRAT: Well, it's not your fault.

MINDY: I remember it so clearly. (She gets up as the light fades on the elevator and rises on the Mindy Scene area.) A lady in the choir sang it and I got chills down my back. I felt Mom pull me so close to her. It was so awesome.

(Everyone freezes as she steps out of the elevator and moves to the scene. The song should begin when Mindy finishes her line.)

Mindy Scene

Mindy and her Mom are seated in two chairs side by side, facing away from the audience. The Singer stands on the riser facing them and begins singing, "I Heard the Bells on Christmas Day." During the final line of music, Mindy returns to the elevator. The light fades from the scene and rises at the elevator as she arrives.

LEWIS: Just you and your mom go?

MINDY: That is my whole family.

LEWIS: You have no brothers or sisters?

MINDY: No.

DRAYTON: Boy, are you lucky.

LEWIS: Where's your dad?

MINDY: I don't have one.

LEWIS: What do you mean? Everybody has a dad. (Turns to Blyth.) Don't they?

BLYTH (shaking her head): Her mother and father didn't get married.

LEWIS (confused): I don't get it.

MINDY: My mom got pregnant when she was sixteen. Then I was born and, well . . . (Smiling.) we've been together since.

DRAYTON (after a slight pause): It's starting to get a little stuffy in here. (Unfastens his jacket.)

16

STRAT: Now that you mention it, it is getting hot in here. *(To Drayton.)* Does it seem like it's harder to breath, Dray?

MINDY: Don't say that, you're scaring me.

BLYTH: Let's not panic here.

LEWIS: Too bad we can't open a door or window or something.

DRAYTON *(smartly to Lewis):* Well, if we could, we wouldn't be in here, now would we?

BLYTH *(to Drayton):* Why are you always so mean?

DRAYTON: I'm stuck in an elevator and I want to get out.

BLYTH: We all do.

MINDY: Maybe we can sing a Christmas carol now.

DRAYTON: Do we have to?

BLYTH: Let's sing something else. Those Christmas songs don't make sense anyway.

STRAT: What do you mean?

BLYTH: The words in them. Peace on earth and stuff. Like the one Mindy just told us about . . . and the songs that army band in the mall were singing. *(She gets up and the light fades on the elevator. The song, "7 O'clock News/Silent Night" begins and all except Blyth freeze.)* They keep singing songs about peace, but I don't see any peace. Where's all the peace on the earth? Look outside. Look in the newspaper. Listen to the radio. *(She moves and stands in front of the white backdrop holding a TV remote control, pointing it towards the audience as if changing channels.)*

Blyth Scene

As Blyth stands, slides are projected on her and the white screen. The slides are chunks of newspaper clips of wars, murders, abuse, etc. They can easily be made by photocopying newspaper clips onto an overhead transparency and then cut to fit a slide frame. Each slide should show only a prominent word in the title and a portion of each article. These slides are shown throughout the song, "7 O'Clock News" which is less than two minutes. Use about twenty slides, each shown at about five seconds each. At the end, Blyth returns to the elevator and the lights rise.

DRAYTON: You make Christmas sound so depressing.

BLYTH: Well, isn't it? It seems kind of phony when they talk about peace at Christmas.

MINDY: Why do we even have it?

(Drayton begins looking at the roof and thinking.)

LEWIS: What?
MINDY: Christmas.
LEWIS: Well . . . because! *(Pause.)* I don't know.
DRAYTON: Well, there's no school. Score one up for that.
STRAT: Maybe it helps boost business for the turkey farmers.
BLYTH: Nah. Shopping. That's what it's all about.
LEWIS *(excited):* You mean for presents?
BLYTH: For everything.
LEWIS: But mostly for the presents. I mean, without presents, Christmas morning just wouldn't be . . . *(Stuck for words.)* wouldn't be . . .
STRAT: Christmas morning.
LEWIS: Yeah.
STRAT: That was always the best part. I could never wait till morning. Don't you guys ever find it hard to sleep on Christmas Eve?
BLYTH: Well, it sure will be this year in this cramped box.
DRAYTON *(still looking up at roof):* You know, if we could get up through the roof, and . . .
BLYTH: Forget it! *(Drayton shows frustration.)* Somebody is going to come and get us. We're just going to have to wait.
STRAT: But what if no one knows we're here?
DRAYTON: Yeah!

(Everyone is quiet. Pause.)

MINDY: My mom and I don't buy gifts.
LEWIS: You don't buy presents at Christmas?
MINDY: We can't afford them, so we make them.
STRAT: Hey, that's kind of cool.
MINDY: Christmas morning is so much fun.
STRAT: It must be pretty special.
LEWIS: We have a rule at our house at Christmastime. "In bed by 10 P.M. . . . stay there till 8 A.M." *(Pauses and smiles.)* Never works, though. Never has.
STRAT: We had a rule like that, too.
LEWIS: You don't anymore?
STRAT: Not since my mom and dad died.
BLYTH: Your mom and dad died?

Stuck in a Box

STRAT: When I was six.

MINDY: Whom do you live with now?

STRAT: My aunt and uncle. They're really nice, but they're not like Mom and Dad. Christmas was so much different then. Just like Lewis was saying . . . it was so hard getting to sleep. And in the morning . . . I drove my mom and dad nuts.

(Everyone freezes and Strat leaves the elevator and moves to the scene during his last line. The light fades and rises as he moves. The song "You Gotta Get Up" begins as he leaves.)

Strat Scene

Strat, reliving being a kid, moves towards the door first and knocks, trying to wake up his parents. When the song refers to reindeer, he moves towards the window, looking through it as if looking outside. He then moves back to the door to finish the song. When the song refers to what his siblings might get, he is at the pile of gifts, snooping through them. Optional: Slides of Christmas morning can be shown on the white backdrop during the musical interlude. At the end, he moves back to the elevator. The light fades as he leaves and rises as he arrives back in the elevator.

DRAYTON: I think I have an idea!

BLYTH: No, wait a minute. *(To Strat.)* What's this stuff about a baby born in . . . what was it?

STRAT: Bethlehem?

DRAYTON: What difference does it make? I have an idea!

BLYTH *(to Strat, ignoring Drayton):* Yeah. What is that?

STRAT: I don't know. I just remember Mom always telling me that stuff at Christmastime.

DRAYTON: Who cares?

BLYTH *(to Drayton):* If it has something to do with this peace on earth stuff, I want to know.

(Drayton sits down in the corner with his head in his hands.)

MINDY *(to Strat):* Hey, yeah . . . you did say peace on earth, didn't you?

STRAT: Yeah, I think so.

LEWIS: How was that again . . . that line? I hope there's peace on earth—goodwill to men—

STRAT: —On account of that baby . . . born in Bethlehem.

BLYTH: Yeah. Who's this baby—and what's a Bethlehem?

DRAYTON (trying to get everyone's attention): Hello! Are we going to try to get out of this elevator?

MINDY (ignoring Drayton): At the Christmas Eve services, they always talk and sing about a baby named Jesus being born in Bethlehem.

LEWIS: I think I know something about that. Wasn't the mom and dad Mary and Bob or Brian or . . . something.

DRAYTON (frustrated): It's Joseph! And there were a bunch of shepherds and three wise guys who brought gifts. There. That's the story. Now, let's get out of here, can we?

BLYTH (to Drayton): Cute. But who asked you?

DRAYTON: I just happen to know the story, okay? Jesus was born in a barn because the inn was packed out. I can't believe you guys haven't heard this before.

STRAT: You know, it's starting to sound familiar.

BLYTH (to Drayton): How would you know all this stuff?

LEWIS: Are you withholding information?

DRAYTON: Look. Who cares? It's just a dumb little story—and it isn't exactly going to get us out of here, so—

STRAT: I do remember that story. I learned about it when I was a kid at church and . . . (Stops, looks at Drayton.) Dray . . . you go to church?

DRAYTON (embarrassed): Why?

BLYTH: You do!

DRAYTON (defensively): My mom makes me.

STRAT (to Drayton): Mary and Joseph went to Bethlehem, right?

DRAYTON: Yeah. They had to so that a census could be taken.

BLYTH: Census?

DRAYTON: Registration. Roll call. (Pause.) Attendance. You know, a head count . . . so that they could pay taxes.

MINDY: Every time we go to the Christmas Eve program, they make such a big deal about this baby. Why is that?

DRAYTON: Because that's what Christmas is—Jesus Christ being born.

LEWIS: So?

DRAYTON: So?! He is the Savior.

LEWIS: Savior?

DRAYTON: Savior. (Thinking.) To save everyone from . . . death. That's where the Heaven and Hell thing comes in. If you believe in Jesus, you go to Heaven. If you don't—well, you know.

STRAT: How come you never told me any of this stuff?

DRAYTON: I don't know. It never seemed all that important.

BLYTH: Hold it. Where does the peace on earth stuff come in here? I'm listening to all this . . . but I didn't hear the word peace in there.

DRAYTON: I feel like I'm in church again. Look. This will take too long.

LEWIS: It's not like we're going anywhere real fast.

BLYTH (to Drayton): Give me the condensed version.

DRAYTON: You've never heard of any of this before?

BLYTH: No.

DRAYTON (to himself): I thought everybody knew this stuff. Okay. Where do I start? God loves us so much, that He sent Jesus to the earth.

MINDY: Wait! I thought Jesus was a baby in a manger.

LEWIS: What's a manger?

MINDY: Beats me.

DRAYTON: Cut! Hold on, will you? Let me tell the story. He had to be born so that He could be human like people on earth. Now . . . because none of us is perfect . . .

BLYTH: Speak for yourself. (Drayton gives her a look of frustration.) Sorry.

DRAYTON: Because none of us is perfect, we can't be close to God. In other words, there's no peace between us and God.

LEWIS: There it is, the "peace" word.

DRAYTON: We're not perfect because we do bad things. The only way we can have peace with God is if we pay for these bad things.

MINDY: How do you pay for that?

DRAYTON: You would have to die.

STRAT: Ouch.

BLYTH: Get real.

DRAYTON: That's why God sent Jesus. First to be born, then to die, then come alive again. When He died, He took our place for our sins.

BLYTH: You're kiddin' me.

DRAYTON: Hang on. That's not all. God says if we have peace with Him, we can have peace inside of ourselves. (Pause.) Now, I was thinking, maybe we can boost someone up through the roof and he can climb to the door of the next floor. (All stare at Drayton, then begin arguing all at once.)

LEWIS: Who's going to do that? I'm not going up!

STRAT: You can't climb up there; it's too dangerous.

BLYTH: You're crazy. How can you open the door from inside?

DRAYTON: It's just an idea and I don't see you suggesting anything.

MINDY (yelling above everyone else): Hello! (All stop and stare at Mindy.)

BLYTH (to Mindy): I didn't know you could talk that loud.

Stuck in a Box

MINDY (*to Blyth*): Only when I have to. (*To all.*) This is not the meaning of peace. Now, if we're going to get out of here, we're going to have to work together. And I think everyone wants to get out—right?

ALL: Yeah . . . right . . . of course . . .

MINDY: Now, I may be jumping to conclusions, but what is that big red knob on the bottom of the control panel that says "Emergency Stop"?

DRAYTON: It's an Emergency Stop button.

BLYTH: Clever, Drayton!

STRAT: It says, "Pull to stop elevator."

DRAYTON: It's been pulled out. Who pulled it out? Louie! (*Points to Lewis.*) That's who.

LEWIS: What? I did not. And if I did, then I don't know how it happened.

BLYTH: It was your fault, Drayton. You're the one who pushed Lewis up against the control panel.

(*Everyone begins arguing at the same time.*)

STRAT: His coat must have got caught on it and pulled it out. I wonder why the phone and bell don't work though.

LEWIS: It was an accident. You can't blame it on me. I didn't even know.

DRAYTON: I told you it was him. We shouldn't have let him on the elevator to begin with.

BLYTH: We wouldn't have got stuck with you on here either, Drayton.

MINDY (*yelling above the others*): Hello again! (*Everyone is quiet again.*) I'm beginning to know the difference between peace on earth and total chaos. (*Pause.*) Who cares whose fault it is? Who cares why the phone and bell didn't work before? Who cares? Why not just try pressing the button and seeing if that's the problem?

BLYTH: Good idea. Strat—push it in.

(*He does and they motion the elevator working again. They all cheer. The door opens at the first floor and Drayton jumps out.*)

DRAYTON: We're free! Come on, Strat. I've got to get going or I'm going to be late. (*They both leave quickly.*)

LEWIS (*begins to leave and then turns back to Blyth and Mindy in the elevator*): Uhhm. Sorry.

BLYTH: It wasn't your fault, Lewis. I'm just glad we got it working again.

LEWIS: Thanks. I've got to get going. (*Leaves.*)

BLYTH: Good thinking, Mindy! (*They hug.*)

MINDY: Well, let's get out of this thing.

Stuck in a Box

BLYTH: Yeah. I'm glad that's over with.

MINDY: Look . . . I've got to hurry and get to the church. Mom's going to be worried if I'm late.

BLYTH: Min . . . would you mind if I came along?

MINDY (surprised): Wow, Blyth. Sure!

BLYTH: I've never even been in a church, so I'm a little nervous. This stuff about a baby and peace on earth sounds interesting, you know?

MINDY: Yeah. I know. Well, come on, let's get going or we'll miss the beginning.

Church lobby scene. Lights fade and upbeat Christmas music plays in between. Possibly "Linus and Lucy," by Vince Guaraldi, from A Charlie Brown Christmas. *Lights up in the church lobby scene. Mindy has a program in hand.*

BLYTH (looking around): Wow. This is kind of neat.

MINDY: Let's wait here until I find my mom.

BLYTH (points to stage right): Mindy. Look! It's Lewis.

(Lewis enters.)

MINDY: Lewis, what are you doing here?

LEWIS: Well, I got to thinking about what you guys were talking about in the elevator. And, I don't know anything about any of that, and I wanted to come and find out.

MINDY: Want to sit with us?

LEWIS: Would it be okay?

MINDY: Sure.

BLYTH: So, Mindy. What happens at these things?

MINDY: We sing Christmas songs and they put on a play.

LEWIS: Cool. What's the play about?

MINDY (looks at her program): It's a story about five kids that get stuck in an elevator. (Pauses while Blyth and Lewis react.) Just kidding. It's usually about the stuff Drayton was talking about.

STRAT (comes up behind them): Blyth, Mindy?

BLYTH: Strat! You too?

MINDY: Did you come to see the play too? Where's Drayton?

STRAT: Well, I was trying to keep up with him and lost him about a block away. I've been searching for him for the last ten minutes. Then I saw you two coming into this church . . . and since I couldn't find Drayton, I thought I'd catch up with you guys. Hope you don't mind.

Stuck in a Box

MINDY: No. This is great, Strat.

STRAT: Drayton said he had somewhere to go, so I'll just catch up with him at his house later.

LEWIS: You want to sit with us?

BLYTH *(looking past Strat to stage left):* I don't believe it!

MINDY: What?

(All turn to see what Blyth is looking at.)

LEWIS: Drayton?

DRAYTON *(enters):* Sorry I lost you, Strat. I didn't want to be late.

BLYTH: Don't tell me you came to see this too.

DRAYTON: No, not really.

STRAT: Then what are you doing here?

DRAYTON *(pausing):* I'm in the play. *(All look at each other and laugh.)* Look guys, I'm sorry for the way I behaved in the elevator.

MINDY/BLYTH: No big deal. Forget it.

DRAYTON: No, really. On my way here, I started thinking about all this information I know about Christmas and Jesus and stuff . . . but it's never seemed real to me . . . until I was telling you about it. Talking to you guys in the elevator about it made me realize I've just been doing and talking church stuff with no reason. It's like I've been stuck in a box. *(Pause.)* Well, anyway. I saw you guys over here and I just wanted to say, "sorry." I've got to go. *(Starts to leave.)*

BLYTH: Hey, Dray. Why don't we all go over to my house after the play?

(The others agree.)

DRAYTON: Yeah, sure. Maybe we can. *(He leaves.)*

MINDY: Hey, there's my mom. Let's go. *(Blyth follows Mindy off.)*

LEWIS: Hey, Strat. Isn't this a neat Christmas Eve? *(Strat chuckles in acknowledgment.)* We should do this again next year. *(Leaves. Strat follows.)*

STRAT: Yeah, sure. But let's skip the elevator part.

(Lights blackout.)

Stuck in a Box

The Bethlehem Miracle

Ruth Powell

Characters and songs they sing:

ANIMALS: "The Friendly Beasts"

STARS: "Jesus Bids Us Shine" and "Shine, Shine, Just Where You Are" or "Beautiful Christmas Star"

ANGELS: "Angels We Have Heard on High"

SHEPHERDS: "While Shepherds Watched Their Flocks"

SHEPHERD BOY

ARRIVING THRONG: "Have You Any Room for Jesus?"

CHOIR: "O Little Town of Bethlehem," "In the Stillness of the Night" and "We Three Kings"

SOLDIERS

VILLAGE WOMEN: "In the Village of Bethlehem" or "The Birthday of a King"

INNKEEPER

INNKEEPER'S WIFE

TAX COLLECTORS

BETHLEHEM PEOPLE: "Beautiful Star of Bethlehem" or "There's a Beautiful Star"

MARY

JOSEPH

THREE WISE MEN

TWO READERS: join Choir in "We Three Kings"

SOLOIST: "Because He Lives"

Also needed: three more innkeepers, sheep and servant (nonspeaking); prop people; light person

Time: approximately thirty minutes

Scenes: Bethlehem street with three inns and a well, stable scene, hillside scene, room scene

Scene 1

Scene opens with Bethlehem street—three inns: The Hotel Bethlehem, Bethlehem Villa, and Bethlehem Inn. A well and stable scene are off to the side. The inns need to be made so people can come and go through the open doorways.

Choir: "O Little Town of Bethlehem" *(first and second stanzas)*

(At the words, "The silent stars go by," there is a quick break in the singing as a group of small children—the Stars—carrying stars aloft, tiptoe dramatically onto the stage.)

Stars: "Jesus Bids Us Shine" *(Edwin O. Excell, Susan Bogert Warner, sing verse only after momentary pause after the Choir stops singing, followed by "Shine, Shine, Just Where You Are" or "Beautiful Christmas Star" then leave stage.)*

(After a brief silence, Village Women emerge from inns going to the well.)

Village Women *(suggested lines):*
1 *(yawning):* I am still tired from all the work we did yesterday!
2: Yes, our masters may not appreciate all we do, but they would be in trouble if we weren't here to do their work for them.
3: Bethlehem's going to be a busy place for the next few days.
4: Bethlehem has always been a special city.
5: I wonder what will happen in our city today, with all the people coming and going.
6: I have the feeling this will be a very special day!

Village Women: "In the Village of Bethlehem" *(two stanzas)* or "The Birthday of a King" *(William Harold Neidlinger)*

Scene 2

Abrupt and noisy appearance of Tax Collectors and Soldiers. Soldiers come in marching, hup, two, three, stopping outside the inns.

First Soldier: Attention! You men move on and find yourselves rooms in the inns around town. Lucas and I will stay here in this inn.

TAX COLLECTOR 1: Well, we're just as important to this operation as you are. Who gives you first rights at the inn? Move aside. We want the best rooms available!

SECOND SOLDIER *(to First Soldier)*: What if we can't find rooms?

FIRST SOLDIER: Then obviously you will sleep outside—put up your tents, spread your sleeping mats. Go on, get moving!

SOLDIER'S ASSISTANT *(to Tax Collectors)*: You miserable tax people, get out of our way. We are Romans!

TAX COLLECTOR 1: Well, we represent Rome!

TAX COLLECTOR 2: We are just as important as you are!

TAX COLLECTOR 3: Let's get to the door ahead of these soldiers and show them who we are!

INNKEEPER *(smoothly)*: Come in, come in, all of you. If you have plenty of money, there is plenty of room!

(Tax Collectors and Soldiers go in, pausing to pay.)

INNKEEPER *(after a few enter)*: What? I charge more than this!! Come back here and give me more money.

THIRD SOLDIER *(stepping back out with sword in hand)*: Here is what I will pay you with if you give us any trouble.

INNKEEPER: Oh! Yes Sir! Right you are, Sir.

(All is silent again. Animals enter, one or several at a time as they sing the animal song, "The Friendly Beasts." They go to the stable area.)

ANIMALS: "The Friendly Beasts"

(After a brief silence, throngs of travelers come down the aisle, jostling and pushing and muttering.)

TRAVELERS *(suggested lines)*:
1: Man, do my feet hurt!
2: I've walked about a hundred miles.
3: Those Romans don't care if we drop dead on the road.
4: That would make fewer people to count.
5: But also fewer taxes to collect.
6: Wonder if the inns will be full.
7: Maybe, but they will probably have room if we have money.
8: Someday they may turn away someone really important.
9 *(with a laugh)*: Well, I doubt they're expecting a king or the Messiah!

CROWD: "Have You Any Room for Jesus?" (*Sung by throng when they reach the stage.*)

(*After song, throng scatters to the inns. Mary and Joseph are at the back of the crowd. They come down the aisle and reach the stage at the song's end. Mary and Joseph go first to one inn, then another. Innkeepers shake their heads and motion them on until they reach the main inn. This is all in pantomime.*)

INNKEEPER (*tired and cross*): Here, here, move on! My inn is full to overflowing with a few customers and a lot of Roman officials. Move on!

JOSEPH: Sir, as you can see, we have passed all the other inns. My wife is exhausted and will soon give birth. Can't you help us?

INNKEEPER: Who am I? Am I a magician that I can make a new room just for you? Move on, I say!

INNKEEPER'S WIFE: Wait! I know what it is to need comfort and help at a time like this. (*To husband.*) James, let's hear no more of this complaining. Send the servant to clear a part of the stable. It won't be a rich room, but it will offer shelter and a place to rest.

(*Servant appears and leads Mary and Joseph to darkened stable area. A brief silence follows, then curtain and scene change, about three minutes.*)

AUDIENCE: "Silent Night! Holy Night"

Scene 3

Hillside outside Bethlehem. Shepherds are sitting around a fire. Large or small group of shepherds, three speak, the rest sing. Small flock of sheep off to the right.

CHOIR: "How Quiet Is the Night" or "In the Stillness of the Night" (*John F. Wilson, Hope Publishing Co.*)

(*Sheep begin baaing softly until shepherds begin to speak.*)

FIRST SHEPHERD: How still the night is! There is no wind and even the sheep are resting quietly. Look at the stars.

SECOND SHEPHERD: I get tired of your being so cheerful when I am sleepy. Looking at stars just makes me want to shut my eyes. Please be quiet!

SHEPHERD BOY: Shh-h-h! Listen!! I hear music.

SECOND SHEPHERD: Music! *(Sarcastically.)* Maybe the stars are singing! Hush. Let me sleep.

SHEPHERDS AND SHEEP: "While Shepherds Watched Their Flocks" *(two stanzas)*

FIRST SHEPHERD *(drops to his knees as Angel appears):* Oh, the Lord be praised!

(Shepherds fall prostrate.)

ANGEL: "Fear not: for, behold I bring you good tidings of great joy, which shall be to all people."

ANGELIC HOST: "For unto you is born this day in the city of David a Saviour, which is Christ the Lord."

ANGELS: "Angels We Have Heard on High" *(sung triumphantly)*

SECOND SHEPHERD *(rising hesitantly):* What wonder is this?

SHEPHERD BOY *(with joy):* We are not sleepy anymore! Come on, let's go.

FIRST SHEPHERD: Indeed we are blessed. God truly sent His angels with glad tidings and even the heavens rang with joy. Come, let us go to Bethlehem.

(Shepherds go and kneel at the stable. Light comes on in the stable. Curtain, three minutes as audience sings.)

AUDIENCE: "Joy to the World"

Scene 4

(Return to original Bethlehem scene. It is early evening. Stable is dark until wise men are ready to enter. Stage is now converted to look like a room, remove manger, use larger child.)

BETHLEHEM PEOPLE *(as though out in the street near the house where Mary and Joseph are, suggested lines):*

1: Look, there's a strange new star.

2: It looks like it's shining right down on that house.

3: How can that be? Who ever heard of a star shining over a particular house?

4: You're always trying to figure out the why of things, Abigail. Let's just enjoy the beauty of the star!

SONG BY BETHLEHEM PEOPLE: "Beautiful Star of Bethlehem" or "There's a Beautiful Star"

5: Well, things have been nice and quiet around here since all that excitement when the people came to enroll for their taxes.

6: Yes, but there are some things that still make me wonder.

7: Speaking of wonder—do you see what is coming down the road!

(Wise men come down the aisle as piano plays softly or group sings.)

CHOIR: "We Three Kings"

FIRST WISE MAN: Did you notice that Herod seemed upset when we told him a new King was born?

SECOND WISE MAN: Yes. I'm not sure what we should do about that. Herod doesn't have a good reputation as a kind and generous man.

THIRD WISE MAN: You're right about that. Yet he seemed so eager for us to find the new king and bring back word. We had better do some serious thinking about this.

FIRST WISE MAN: I believe that He who placed the star before us, will guide us in what we should do. Come! The star has stopped over this little house. Let us go in.

TWO READERS: Matthew 2:9-11 *(Readers taking turns reading.)*

(Wise men do actions to follow Scripture. Remain for final tableau. Room is lighted for Wise men's entrance.)

READERS *(in unison):* God sent His Son. Let us rejoice in Him!

SOLOIST: "Because He Lives" *(first and second stanzas)*

Auditions
V. Louise Cunningham

Characters:
TRAVIS, talent manager
BEN, a speaker
TERRY, a teacher
SUE, a singer
CONRAD, a humble man
DORA, a dancer
JIM, big production manager
TERRY'S cast includes: MARY, JOSEPH, CHILDREN to sing
JIM'S cast includes: MARY, JOSEPH, YOUNG CHILD, WISE MEN
CHOIR (optional)

Setting: Audition hall

Time: Present

Costumes: Modern day and biblical style robes

Props: Big mirror or shiny wrap stretched to look like a mirror, positioned between two lights that can be flashed; a machine that dispenses numbers; an entry door; two tape recorders; a manger

Scriptures taken from the *New International Version* of the Bible.

Scene 1

Ben, Dora, Sue, Terry and Conrad are on stage waiting for their turns. Jim enters.

JIM: I see there is quite a group here already. I hope this doesn't take very long. I have a lot of people involved with my act and after all this is the Christmas season, and everyone is very busy.
DORA: You need to take a number.
JIM: Take a number?

DORA: The machine is over there. *(She points to the machine.)* You pull out a slip of paper with a number and we are called in order.

SUE: I'm number three.

JIM: What is it you do?

SUE: I'm a singer. I'm sure that when they hear me, I will be chosen.

TERRY: How can you be so sure? After all, I have all my students here and everyone adores to watch children in a Christmas pageant.

JIM: I'm sure they can't compare with my group of talented artists over there. Everyone in my group has been in road shows and has played on Broadway.

BEN: Well, *(Standing up and deepening voice.)* well, with all my elocution lessons, I'm sure that after my simple telling of the Christmas story, I will be chosen. I have brought tears to the eyes of the faithful. *(Sits back down.)*

DORA: Excuse me, but are those camels?

JIM: Well, of course. The wise men didn't have sports utility vehicles to travel in back then. Check out their costumes. Wardrobe did an excellent job of outfitting them, don't you think? So what do you do?

DORA: I dance.

SUE: I don't see how that fits into the Christmas story. Some churches frown on dancing, so I think you might as well go home.

DORA: You don't understand. Our group dances in the Irish fashion that has been so popular. We tap very fast and we beat out the rhythm of some of the old Christmas carols. Listen to this. *(Starts to tap.)*

SUE: Well, it is different from modern dancing which is so . . .

BEN: Visual? *(Stands.)* But I think it is much more beneficial if words are used. *(Deepens voice.)* After all, what if they don't know the songs? *(Sits down.)*

DORA *(unsure of herself)*: I guess they could use an overhead and put the words on a screen.

JIM: So, what exactly do the children do? Maybe I could incorporate them into my group.

TERRY: It looks like you have a huge group already.

JIM: Oh, well, your choice. How about you? *(Speaks to Conrad.)*

CONRAD: I'm a contrite heart.

JIM: But what do you do?

CONRAD: I'm just here.

BEN: But you must do something or why did you come?

CONRAD: I don't do anything. I brought myself to please the King.

JIM: O—kay. (*Turns away and then back.*) Perhaps I could try to find a part for you in my production. (*Pause.*) You could be a camel boy.
SUE: Do you sing?
CONRAD: Not really.
TERRY: I could fit him in with my students.
BEN (*stands*): That is something to consider. I could help you learn how to speak.
JIM: A camel boy doesn't have to do much.
DORA (*looking at watch*): Isn't it about time for the auditions to begin?

(*Sue checks her hair again in the mirror.*)

TRAVIS (*enters*): Good morning.
ALL: Good morning.
TRAVIS: Through the very doors I came through, one of you or your group may enter to MEET THE KING.

(*All gasp.*)

TRAVIS: As you know, I've called an audition to see who or what group can best tell the Christmas story. Whatever you do, the main focus is to glorify the King. (*Pointing to the mirror.*) This mirror is actually a two-way window. Sometimes the person I work for comes and watches and sometimes he relies on my judgments. The light on the left flashes if you don't make it. The light on the right flashes if you and your act are selected.

(*Sue backs away from the mirror she has been standing by and looks embarrassed. Dora gives a timid wave toward the mirror.*)

TRAVIS: Hand me your business card before you begin. You have all taken a number I'm sure. Who is first?
DORA: I am. (*Turns on tape recorder, which doesn't work. She gets very flustered.*) It was working just a minute ago. (*Tries again.*)
BEN (*stands and says in a deep voice*): Is it plugged in? (*Goes to look and sits down.*) It should work.
DORA: Yes, it is plugged in.
TRAVIS: Can you tell me what you wanted to do?
DORA: Not very well. You see, I tap dance to Christmas carols. The way I tap identifies the song. (*Taps very briefly.*) I'm sorry, it's no use. I'll leave.

("No" light flashes.)

JIM: No, stay. Perhaps I can use you in my production. Let me think about it.

TRAVIS: Next.

BEN *(stands and poses, in a deep voice):* I believe that would be me. *(Gives his card to Travis.)* I tell the Christmas story. "In the beginning was the Word, and the Word was with God, and the Word was God. He was with God in the beginning. Through him all things were made; without him nothing was made that has been made. In him was life, and that life was the light of men. The light shines in the darkness, but the darkness has not understood it" (John 1:1-5). *(Pause.)* "In those days Caesar Augustus issued a decree that a census should be taken of the entire Roman world. (This was the first census that took place while Quirinius was governor of Syria.) And everyone went to his own town to register. So Joseph also went up from the town of Nazareth in Galilee to Judea, to Bethlehem the town of David, because he belonged to the house and line of David. He went there to register with Mary, who was pledged to be married to him and was expecting a child. While they were there, the time came for the baby to be born, and she gave birth to her firstborn, a son. She wrapped him in cloths and placed him in a manger, because there was no room for them in the inn" (Luke 2:1-7).

TRAVIS: That was fine. *(Looks at paper in hand.)* Ben.

("No" light flashes.)

JIM: Too bad, you have a great speaking voice.

BEN *(sits down):* I think I'll stay and watch the rest if that is okay?

TRAVIS: That's okay as long as there is room. Next.

(Sue hands her card to Travis and walks to her tape recorder.)

DORA: I hope her recorder works.

(Music comes on. Sue sings a song relating to shepherds, such as "Angels, from the Realms of Glory," "It Came upon the Midnight Clear," "Hark! the Herald Angels Sing" or "While Shepherds Watched Their Flocks.")

TERRY: That was beautiful.

("No" light flashes.)

BEN: I'm surprised. That was lovely.
TRAVIS: I'm sorry. Next.

(Terry hands her card and ushers children in. They group around two children playing Mary and Joseph. They sing "Away in a Manger.")

DORA: Weren't they too precious!

(All look at light as it flashes "No.")

JIM: The students did so well. I believe I'm next. *(Hands Travis his card and addresses his response to the mirror.)* I take up the story when Jesus was a young child and He and Mary and Joseph are living in a house. The three wise men come. Yuk, get that camel out of here before it spits again!
SUE *(points off to one side):* Oh, dear, look at the mess one of the camels is leaving.
TERRY: But the costumes of the wise men are exquisite.
JIM: I'm sorry. We'll just leave the camels out and I'll set the stage. *(Puts people in place. There are Mary, Joseph, young child, wise men with very elaborate gifts. A choir can sing "We Three Kings" while he arranges the people.)*

(All look at lights. "No" light flashes.)

TERRY: I can't believe it. Everything was just beautiful.
BEN *(stands):* Sorry, old man, I thought it was great.
TRAVIS: I guess that is all of you for today.
DORA: No, there is one more, Conrad.
TRAVIS: And what do you do? *(He takes card from Conrad.)*
CONRAD: I give myself, and a contrite heart.
TRAVIS: I don't understand.
CONRAD: I don't mean to disparage anyone's talent or gift that was brought to display before the King at this Christmas season. I think the beauty and motion of a dancer expresses a lot and I'm sorry we didn't get to see Dora's special dance. You can tell I don't have the deep voice or eloquence to tell a story like Ben, and he did choose the most wonderful story in history. When I sing, animals cringe, though I admire greatly those who can. It's too bad about

the camels, but it is hard to work with animals. They are so unpredictable. Sometimes riches and costly gifts like the wise men brought are a poor substitute for heartfelt gifts. I bring myself and a contrite heart.

TRAVIS: How can you show me a contrite heart?

CONRAD: I can't really, but the King would know.

TRAVIS: That's true. For now, why don't you talk to me a little and it might help others.

CONRAD: I'll try. I would like to share my thoughts about Christmas. *(He pulls out a sheet of paper.)* If we can truly look at the manger, the life of Jesus, what He did on the cross, and seek Him and all His glory, it gives us the proper perspective. Then at Christmas we can remember this. Christmas isn't giving expensive jewelry, it's the Crown of Life. Christmas isn't books, but the Word of Life. Christmas isn't gadgets, it's our Savior and Lord. Christmas isn't stuffed animals, it's the Lamb of God. Christmas isn't casserole dishes, but the Bread of Life. Christmas isn't a flocked tree, but the cross of Calvary. Christmas is a time of concentrating on who Christ is. It is a time to focus on the birth of Christ. Christmas is a time for more prayer and meditation on Scripture. Christmas is a time to pray that God will bring those people around your tree He wants there and for your acceptance of His will.

(All gasp as "Yes" light flashes. Conrad hands paper to Travis before he walks through the door.)

BEN: Wow! He's going through the door!

SUE: I wish I could audition again. This time I'd sing for His honor and glory and not my own. It would be my gift to Him.

BEN: I know what you mean. I was so full of myself and how I sounded and where I put my inflections, I forgot I was telling how God came to earth.

(Dora leans down and starts changing shoes.)

JIM: Why are you taking off your tap shoes?

DORA: I realize I don't have to perform or do anything to meet the King.

TERRY: I was sitting here thinking about how to speed up arranging the children to sing "Away in a Manger" when I should be more concerned about making sure they know the Baby in the manger.

36

They need to know that it is God in the manger and that He came as a king. They need to know Jesus as their Savior while their hearts are still tender.

DORA: That's a nice thought. I wonder where can we get a contrite heart?

TRAVIS: Conrad handed me a copy of this for each of you. *(Hands them out.)*

JIM: Wow. I can see, with a heart like that, why Conrad was chosen.

TERRY: Why don't you read this to us, Ben?

BEN *(with a more humble spirit):* "What is more, I consider everything a loss compared to the surpassing greatness of knowing Christ Jesus my Lord, for whose sake I have lost all things. I consider them rubbish, that I may gain Christ" (Philippians 3:8). If we live in a mansion and have servants to wait on us, but don't know God, we have nothing. If we own the world's most famous paintings and sculptures, but live without God, we are penniless. If we have tennis courts, swimming pools, saunas, but aren't aware of God, we are destitute. If priceless antiques fill our rooms, rare books line the shelves, but we don't recognize God, we live in poverty. If our clothes are all designer made, our safes full of jewels and yet we live without God, we are beggars. If we dine on gourmet food using fine china and crystal, but don't see God, we are poor. I for one am rich! I know the living eternal God!

DORA: This gives me a whole new meaning to knowing God.

JIM: I realize I need to think more deeply than I have about spiritual matters.

TERRY: That was beautiful.

SUE: I am rich and didn't realize it.

TRAVIS: I think you are all beginning to see what would please the King of kings whose birth we celebrate at this time of the year. Too often we try to do things or put on a good show, when all God wants from us is a broken and contrite heart. When your hearts are ready, you can all meet the King.

(Lights out.)

CONGREGATION: "I Surrender All" *(or similar song)*

Auditions

No Room at the Ritz

Roberta Robertson

This play blends the familiar, traditional story of "No Room at the Inn" with modern-day circumstances. The Joseph and Mary become the poor of our day. You'll be surprised at the ending and motivated to open yourself to receive the One who knocks at the door of your heart. Maybe there is room after all.

Cast:
JOE—a poor, middle-aged man
MARY ANN—wife of Joe, pregnant, due in a few days
MAN—Jesus, an older, wealthy father
CHILDREN'S CHOIR—K-6th grade, can be small or large group
CHILD—six years old
MRS. DISALVO—choir director
TEENAGERS—three to five boys and girls
TWO BELLMEN—in their early twenties
YOUNG CHILDREN'S CHOIR—two-to four-year-olds
CHOIR DIRECTOR—for young Children's Choir (nonspeaking)
WEALTHY COUPLE—yuppie type
TWO HOTEL CLERKS—front desk, can add one more as an extra
COUPLE—get the last room
WAITER—for room service
EXTRAS—Scene 1, audience members and hotel representative. Scene 2, other hotel guests, extra hotel employees optional
OPTIONAL NARRATOR—for blackouts

Synopsis of Scenes:
Scene 1—Young Children's Choir caroling outside the hotel
Scene 2—The busy lobby at the front desk
Scene 3—Room 1, The wealthy couple exchanging gifts
Scene 4—Room 2, Teens partying
Scene 5—Room 3, Children's Choir rehearsing
Scene 6—Room 4, The older wealthy man
Scene 7—The Call

Before you begin: Decide beforehand how elaborate you would like your production to be, then keep everything in that perspective. As for the room scenes, they are very similar and can be flopped side to side on the stage, scene to scene. Consider splitting the stage for ease, with the exception of Scene 6. The production time is about thirty minutes.

All Scripture references are from the *New International Version.*

Props and Scenes: lapel microphones, spotlights, holiday decorations (outdoor, scene 1, indoor scenes 2-7)
outdoor winter apparel, (scenes 1, 5)
indoor winter apparel, telephones (scenes 2-7)
luggage (scene 1 particularly); packages (scenes 1, 2)
Christmas gifts (all scenes, particularly scene 3)
computer screen, back view or something comparable; front desk counter (table top); telephones 2; nice front bench to sit on with tall beautiful vase and fresh flower arrangement atop table, situated either behind bench, or if bench is rounded or curved, then in its center—front desk is upstage left of bench (scene 2)
diamond ring (impostor) wrapped in nice little box; bottle of champagne; bar glasses; hors d'oeuvres tray; table; Santa hat (scene 3)
cigarettes; beer bottles; television (scene 4)
birthday cake and candles, tea service, cups, spoons, sugar, milk, lemon (scene 6)

Sound Effects: jingling bells, phones ringing, background laughter and soft holiday music (lobby, scene 2), door knocking, crackling fire, teen heavy metal music

Blackouts—The blackouts at the end of most scenes are symbolic of man's state without God. He is lost. During the blackout we hear man's emptiness. Jesus said, "The man who walks in the dark does not know where he is going" (John 12:35). The rooms represent the places we go for answers. The Scripture verses following the lines spoken in the dark give the answer to that emptiness and are for the use of the director and cast. They are intended as a motivational platform and will hopefully impact those who study them. "My word that goes out from my mouth: It will not return to me empty, but will accomplish what I desire and achieve the purpose for which I sent it" (Isaiah 55:11). For an added effect, these Scriptures may be read aloud, by the Man's voice, after a dramatic pause, following the actors' lines.

Scene 1

The play opens outside the hotel. The young Children's Choir is caroling. Song choice should be simple and up to the discretion of the worship leader and director. The young Children's Choir Director is leading them. Extras can be the audience. The majority are related to the children. A few of the family members may wave at some of the children. After the performance, one person representing the hotel, dressed appropriately, shakes hands with the Choir Director in appreciation. After the children are finished singing, they exit stage right. Audience (extras) applauds.

Scene 2

Scene opens in the busy lobby at the front desk. Phones are ringing. People are coming and going, carrying packages, suitcases, on the way to their rooms, etc. The lobby is decorated for the holidays. Soft music is playing in the background. A couple is at the desk asking for a room. Two Bellmen are standing by the door talking and laughing.

CLERK 1 *(standing, talking on the phone)*: Thank you for calling the Ritz Carlton. How may I direct your call? One moment please. Thank you for calling the Ritz Carlton. How may I direct your call?
CLERK 2 *(standing)*: Okay, the only rooms we have available are our suites. *(Checking paperwork or computer screen.)* We have one left . . . for how many nights do you need this room?
COUPLE *(together)*: Two nights.
CLERK 2: You are in luck; we had a cancellation.

(Couple responds with joy. Clerk 2 gets information from them. They give their credit card, etc. Bellman opens the door for Mary Ann and Joe to enter. Joe thanks him. Mary Ann and Joe are obviously tired. He helps her over to the seats in the center of the lobby.)

JOE: There we go, Mary Ann. That's much better now.
MARY ANN *(sits down)*: Oh, Joseph! This is such a lovely place! I do believe it's out of our price range, though. How nice of those handsome, young men to open the door for us.
(Ticked off Bellmen walk to center stage just past Joe and Mary Ann and stop.)

BELLMAN 1 *(pointing to Joe and Mary Ann)*: Who them?
BELLMAN 2: That's them. The only thing they gave me was a "thank you."

BELLMAN 1 (*in reference to them*): It's called a "tip" you cheap . . .
BELLMAN 2: Don't even waste your time on riffraff like them.
BELLMAN 1 AND 2 (*imitating the actor Jim Carey*): Yeah, ya Loo-h-
   oosers!! (*Both laugh and walk offstage right.*)
JOE (*naively*): What fine young men, Mary Ann.
MARY ANN: Yes, indeed.
JOE: Mary Ann, I'll be right back. Stay here. (*He goes to front desk.*)
   Pardon me, can I get a room here? (*Politely.*) It's probably too
   costly, but . . .

(*No one has time to help him. Finally, Clerk 1 notices him as she is on hold
on the phone.*)

CLERK: I'm sorry, Sir, we don't have any rooms available. These rooms
   have been sold out for months. Sometimes you can get lucky if we get
   a cancellation, as this couple has, but may I suggest booking in ad-
   vance for next time? (*Her call goes through now and she turns from Joe.*)

(*People are walking by. They look down on Joe because of his appearance.
He decides to look anywhere in the hotel for someone to help him. He starts
walking toward an imaginary hallway and ends up offstage.*)

JOE: Excuse me; can you tell me where I might find a room? My wife,
   she's pregnant. Do you know of another hotel nearby . . .

(*He's ignored.*)

BLACKOUT

JOE: We have nowhere to go. Can somebody help us? Please . . .
OPTIONAL NARRATION: "The Son of Man came to seek and save what
   was lost" (Luke 19:10).

(*From this point on, we see different rooms of the hotel where Joe goes to
find anyone who can direct him.*)

Scene 3

*Room 1, the Wealthy Couple. This scene opens with romantic Christmas
music playing, jazz or something slow and nonreligious. There is a bottle of
champagne on the table, there can be a fire in the fireplace if you can be more*

elaborate in your sets. The man is wearing a Santa hat. The woman is open-ing a gift, a diamond ring. She is very excited and tries it on admiringly.

WIFE: Wait now, it's YOUR turn. *(Goes to get his gift.)* Close your eyes. *(Hears a knock on the door, acts like she knows who it is, thinking maybe it's room service or some other delightful surprise.)* Ah-aha, wonder what other little surprises you have for me.

(Husband looks puzzled. She gets up and answers the door. Joe is standing there.)

WIFE *(irritated):* Who are you?
JOE: My name is Joe, . . . Joseph really . . .
WIFE *(cuts him off):* Ha! *(Snidely.)* Where's Mary? *(Laughs.)*
JOE: She's . . .
WIFE *(cuts him off again):* What do you want?

(Husband gets up and comes over to door also.)

JOE *(nervously):* Well, my wife is pregnant and we thought we might be able to get a room here, but they're full—and I was just wondering if . . .
HUSBAND *(to wife):* Honey, I'll handle this, go into the other room. Excuse me, does this look like the front desk? I don't know how you got in here, but I think you better leave as quickly as possible. Do you know what night this is? You must have an awful lot of nerve disturbing people on Christmas Eve! Either that or you're an absolute fool or something. Now I suggest you leave before I call security.
JOE *(astonished):* You misunderstand me Sir. I don't want anything—I was just wondering if you might know of another place to go on this winter night.
WIFE *(from background):* Go see the desk clerk! Can't you understand you're bothering us?
HUSBAND: We just can't help you. We're sorry; again, it's Christmas Eve! Everything is probably taken. *(Shuts door in his face.)*
WIFE *(calls security):* Yes, there is a transient wandering the halls, knocking on doors, and he's just tried to get into our room . . .

BLACKOUT

WIFE *(flustered):* You can't be too careful these days. I mean, he could've . . . well, let's just say I was afraid for my life!

No Room at the Ritz

OPTIONAL NARRATION: "Whoever finds his life will lose it, and whoever loses his life for my sake will find it" (Matthew 10:39).

Scene 4

Room 2. Teens partying. This scene is abstract. Colored flashing lights could be used effectively to portray chaos. There is loud music playing from the television music videos. There are beer cans in the room. Spoiled teens are dancing, bumping into each other. Some can pretend to be smoking.

TEEN 1: Give me a cigarette.
TEEN 2: No way, get your own.
TEEN 1: C'mon, Jerk. I'm serious.
TEEN 2: You owe me so bad! You should just be glad you're here. You got invited to party with the one, the only, party animal in the valley, JIMMAY *(slang for Jimmy)* LEE.

(Knock at the door. There is no answer.)

TEEN 3: Yeah, as long as your parents don't walk in . . .
TEEN 2: Look, I told you, they're gone for a couple days.

(Knock on the door again. The room goes silent.)

BLACKOUT

TEEN 4: Shh-h . . . Did you hear somebody knocking?
TEEN 2: No way! And even if I did, I wouldn't answer.
TEEN 1: I would as long as they had food with 'em. . .

OPTIONAL NARRATION: "All man's efforts are for his mouth, yet his appetite is never satisfied" (Ecclesiastes 6:7).

Scene 5

Room 3. Children's Choir rehearsal. This scene opens inside another hotel room. Some of the children have cookie crumbs and punch stains around their mouths. They are about to rehearse one last time before their long-awaited performance, the special tree-lighting ceremony on the roof. They have been chosen to sing as the tree is raised. Everyone is very excited and energetic. The Choir Director, Mrs. DiSalvo, is a bit on the stressed side.

CHILD (*holding cookie*): Mrs. DiSalvo, I don't feel so good.

MRS. DISALVO: What's the matter?

CHILD (*rubbing stomach*): It's my tummy.

MRS. DISALVO: Oh, it must be too many cookies and punch! How many did you have?

CHILD: Only eight.

MRS. DISALVO: All right. All right, boys and girls. Shh-h . . . I need your attention. It's almost time for the Christmas tree-lighting ceremony on the roof!

CHILD (*whines*): But Mrs. DiSalvo, I'm scared to go on the roof!

MRS. DISALVO: We're not going on the roof boys and girls. The tree is on the roof, but we'll be on the ground in front of the hotel. Now! Let's rehearse one last time!

(*The children rush up to their places. They are pushing and shoving a little. They sing the desired number of songs. No more than two seems best, not to lose the continuity of the play. When they are through singing, they rush out the door and shove Joe out of their way.*)

MRS. DISALVO (*checks her watch*): Oh! Look at the time!

JOE: Can you help me?

MRS. DISALVO (*harriedly*): Boys and girls, wait . . . (*to Joe*) I'm sorry . . . Wait . . . Children, I'm not going to keep reminding you!

(*They leave in disorderly fashion as Joe stands there watching.*)

BLACKOUT

MRS. DISALVO (*sighs*): Life is so overwhelming at times.

OPTIONAL NARRATION: "My heart took delight in all my work, and this was the reward for all my labor. Yet when I surveyed all that my hands had done and what I had toiled to achieve, everything was meaningless, a chasing after the wind; nothing was gained under the sun" (Ecclesiastes 2:10, 11).

Scene 6

Room 4. The older Wealthy Man. Inside this room hope is born. This is the climax of the play. It should be played sincerely, carefully, in love. This man is powerful and lonely for his children. That is all that is on his mind. He is generous, patient and kind. He is wearing a beautiful, long, velvet robe over lounging pajamas, and nice jewelry, maybe a ring and gold bracelet. We can tell at first glance he is wealthy. We see him from the back during most of the scene. The room should be quiet, also with a fire and its crackling sounds. The lighting should be soft and warm. There is a sofa, which Joe and Mary Ann will occupy, facing a chair. The sofa faces the audience. The Man sits in the chair which is not quite center stage. (A chair arrangement would also work.) There is a knock at the door. The Man answers the door. Joe is standing there and suddenly Mary Ann rushes up to Joe.*

MARY ANN *(emotionally):* There you are! I was worried. Oh, Joe don't bother these people. Sir. . . . Oh, Joe you are intruding on a very important man. We are so sorry, sorry to bother you.
MAN: It's no trouble at all. Please come in, both of you. What can I do for you?

(They enter the room awkwardly. Mary is giving Joe looks for overstepping boundaries. Joe thinks they will be leaving momentarily, so it does not concern him. Mary doesn't quite know what Joe's been doing this whole time.)

JOE: Thank you, kind Sir. We won't keep you.
MAN: Actually, I am quite happy that you are here.
JOE AND MARY ANN: You are?
MAN: Yes! Now before you tell me what business brings you here, may I offer you some hot tea? It's . . .
MAN AND MARY ANN: Decaffeinated?
MARY ANN *(smiles):* That would be wonderful! Thank you!

(Man pours tea into cups and gives them to Joe and Mary Ann. They each add sugar, lemon, and/or milk as they continue.)

JOE: Yes, thank you. May God reward you for your generosity.
MAN *(to Joe):* You remind me of my father.

(Joe and Mary Ann chuckle.)

MAN: Have you eaten dinner?
JOE: We are just fine. We are already intruding on your evening. You see, we were hoping to find a place to rest our weary souls. My wife, Mary Ann, she is, as you can see, with child and the baby seems to be coming earlier than expected.

No Room at the Ritz

MAN: Not tonight!

MARY ANN: Oh, no! I don't think so.

MAN (*relieved*): Whew!

JOE: Her doctor believes she will deliver in these next few days, though. We had to make this trip but failed to make hotel reservations. We are simple folks and didn't realize that it is the busiest time here in the valley.

MAN: Yes, it is a busy time of the year here. It seems that everyone is too busy. There is so little time for peace.

MARY ANN: Peace? I think that's a word that's become used up on all the Christmas cards and now there's none left! Although, it's a strange thing, I feel it now.

JOE (*bewildered*): So do I.

MAN: So . . .

JOE: Oh! Pardon me for not introducing myself. My name is Joe. Joe Carpenter. And this is my wife, Mary Ann.

MAN: So good to meet you. You know, I am a people person. I love people.

(*They all laugh.*)

MARY ANN: How can some people be so warm and caring while others are not?

JOE: It's a choice, dear Mary Ann, a choice.

MAN: People have many choices to make. And speaking of choices, you may have my room this evening.

(*Joe and Mary Ann gasp.*)

JOE: Absolutely not! We wouldn't hear of it!

MARY ANN: We could never . . . I can't imagine taking your very bed, dear man.

JOE: This must be why no one would talk to me before; maybe they thought I was after their rooms!

MARY ANN: Joseph! You were knocking on other people's doors? (*Shakes head in shame.*)

MAN: I have many places to go, many homes. I simply came to town to see my children, but they have other business it seems, and cannot see me. I shall not be here for very long. In fact, I may as well go this evening.

JOE: Can this be? You would give to us—strangers—your very own beautiful room and yourself be put out? I mean, someone of your success with so many places to be? It is unusual that you have time to spend on our trivial affairs.

MAN: Trivial? Ha! Most of what is going on in this hotel this evening could be called trivial! Your affairs are quite important to me, as a matter of fact. I care that you have nowhere to lie down this cold evening. Besides, I know just how you feel.

JOE: What were the chances of our finding you? God must be with us!

MARY ANN: Tell us more about you! Tell us of your children.

MAN: I have many children, sons and daughters, many are adopted.

MARY ANN: Adopted? It takes special parenting to care for someone else's children.

MAN: Oh no, they are mine! I love them all the same. Sometimes it hurts when I see them acting as though they belong to someone else. Sometimes they do forget me. Still I would do anything for any one of them. I would even give my life.

MARY ANN (caressing her stomach slightly): I hope that our child is caring . . . like you.

JOE: Maybe your children don't know that you are here, in town.

MAN: They do not return my calls.

MARY ANN: Maybe they feel ashamed; maybe something has happened in their lives.

JOE: Maybe they feel that they have let you down, that they couldn't live up to your expectations, a man such as yourself.

MAN: May it never be! I know that they have made mistakes and will keep making mistakes. It is the human nature. But this is why I have come—to tell them how much I love them! I want to help them, but they don't ask.

MARY ANN: Well, there is still hope! Maybe tonight they will call you.

JOE: Yes! Yes! It is Christmas Eve. Maybe they will give their father the best gift of all, themselves.

MARY ANN: What a Christmas that would be! A real merry Christmas. (Man is so full of joy at this thought. They all begin to hug each other, exclaiming, "Merry Christmas.")

MAN (standing): Oh! I almost forgot. It is my birthday. Will you celebrate my birthday with me?

(Joe and Mary Ann are flattered and agree as a knock on the door is heard. They stand. It is room service. The Waiter comes into the room singing and carrying a birthday cake with lit candles.)

No Room at the Ritz   47

JOE AND MARY ANN *(sing):* Happy birthday to you ... happy birthday to you ...

(Man turns around on this next line. At this point the other actors enter from the same door as the Waiter. The children from the choirs may be on the sides of the stage and all join in to sing the last few lines. Only Joe, Mary Ann, choirs, choir directors and some of the hotel employees are happy. The rest sing with blank stares.)

ENTIRE CAST: Happy birthday, dear Jesus ... happy birthday to You!

(When the Man turns around, we see his nail-scarred hands. He is very happy, smiling, and laughing. The lights begin to dim as the smile turns serious on the Man's face. Everyone else is silent. There is now a spotlight over the Man. He reaches out to the audience with his arms before him.)

Scene 7

MAN: """Here I am! I stand at the door and knock. If anyone hears my voice and opens the door, I will come in and eat with him and he with me. Come to me, all you who are weary and burdened, and I will give you rest. Take my yoke upon you and learn from me, for I am gentle and humble in heart, and you will find rest for your souls. For my yoke is easy and my burden is light" (Revelation 3:20; Matthew 11:28).

(Dramatic pause then blackout. Follow with closing remarks and appropriate song. If your church has special music, this is the time to include it.)

Scripture References: John 1:12-14; Ecclesiastes 2:22; Psalm 29:11; John 17:23; Joshua 24:15; John 14:2, 3; Proverbs 1:28; 1 John 3:16; Proverbs 27:24; Psalm 144:3; Matthew 8:20; Jeremiah 29:13; Psalm 146:9; Luke 2:10, 11; Ephesians 3:18; Isaiah 53:3, 6; John 10:17, 18; Proverbs 28:13; Romans 3:23; Luke 10:16; Proverbs 23:18; Psalm 22:5

Ready for Christmas

Betty Huitema

A program of joy and peace suitable for a candlelight service.

Cast:
NARRATOR (may be minister)
SPEAKERS 1 AND 2 (may be male or female who are good speakers)

Suggested Music: "What Child Is This?"; "The First Noel"; "Thou Didst Leave Thy Throne"; "Redeeming Love"; "He Started the Whole World Singing"; "How Great Our Joy!"; "I Heard the Bells on Christmas Day"; "Lo, How a Rose E'er Blooming"; "Ring the Bells"; "We Three Kings of Orient Are"; "O Holy Night!"; "O Come, All Ye Faithful"; "Silent Night! Holy Night!" *(These songs are found in the hymnal "Worship His Majesty" published by Gaither Music Company, Inc. Other songs may be substituted if director desires.)*

NARRATOR: "The Word became flesh and made his dwelling among us. We have seen his glory, the glory of the One and Only, who came from the Father, full of grace and truth" (John 1:14, *New International Version*). Are you ready for Christmas? Undoubtedly, many of you have been asked this question in the last few days. But what does it really mean to be ready for Christmas?

SPEAKER 1: I like to think of it in terms of getting ready to welcome an important guest to my house. Naturally I would make many preparations. For instance, I would make sure the house would be clean, and I would put on my best clothes. Then I would watch my manners and act appropriately for the occasion to make sure I would not embarrass myself. I would also be looking forward to spending time with this individual and exchanging ideas. You might call it "always being prepared for service."

SPEAKER 2: Great explanation, but what does that have to do with being ready for Christmas? In my opinion, "being ready" means going out and buying presents, then making sure these are wrapped and placed underneath the Christmas tree all set for Christmas morning. I would expect baked goodies, so traditional to the season, and a further "must" is a turkey with all the trimmings for our Christmas dinner. When all these things are taken care of, I feel I am ready for Christmas.

SPEAKER 1: Granted these things are nice. They give us a sense of pleasure, but I believe there is much more to celebrating Christmas. It is easy to get sidetracked, especially when you are influenced by what goes on around you: Christmas carols blaring over loudspeakers to the accompaniment of busy cash registers. In some ways the world has grasped the importance of the "Christ child," although materialistically, much more than Christians. They decorate the stores with glitter and lights, placing a Santa right alongside a nativity scene, thus trying to appeal to everyone. The nativity scene has been glamourized so that no one would think of it as a dirty stable in which animals are found.

NARRATOR: God says in His Word: "But when the fulness of the time was come, God sent forth his Son" (Galatians 4:4, *King James Version*).

CONGREGATION: "What Child Is This?" *(stanzas 1 and 2)*

SPEAKER 1: It was the worst of times for the Jews. They loathed the Romans, who occupied their land; they sighed under their cruel "yoke." Yet it was the best of times for Almighty God to initiate His plan of salvation for mankind. The same Romans provided a network that allowed the "Good News" to be spread far and wide. In order to make the Jewish nation "ready" for the Savior, God sent someone "to prepare the way."

NARRATOR: "There came a man who was sent from God; his name was John. He came as a witness to testify concerning that light, so that through Him all men might believe. He himself was not the light; he came only as a witness to the light. The true light that gives light to every man was coming into the world" (John 1:6-9, *New International Version*).

CONGREGATION: "The First Noel" *(stanzas 2 and 4)*

SPEAKER 1: God wanted the hearts of men and women to be prepared. That is why He sent John the Baptist. He could have arranged for a palace for His Son; instead He chose a stable. To God the Father, who regards the heart of mankind as the most important, the outward appearances and trimmings, of which we are so fond, became secondary.

Speaker 2: And you think that we spent too much time in preparation of the external trimmings rather than preparing our hearts for His coming?

Speaker 1: At this time, yes. I believe that it should be noticeable that we are preparing a feast that honors our Savior. He should be the main focus of our celebration, the great Gift sent from Heaven to earth. Our gifts to others are but a mere reflection of this.

Speaker 2: How do we go about that?

Speaker 1: By asking the Lord to look at our hearts, and point out those attitudes that are contrary to His will and way. By asking Him to forgive our sins, to empty us completely of self and have Jesus come alive in our hearts, accepting Him as our Lord and Savior, so that He can fill us with His love, joy and peace.

Congregation: "Thou Didst Leave Thy Throne" *(stanzas 1 and 5)*

Narrator: "For God so loved the world, that he gave his only begotten Son, that whosoever believeth in him should not perish, but have everlasting life" (John 3:16, *King James Version*).

Narrator: "His Love . . . Reaching" *(A reading, on page 150 written by Gloria Gaither or another appropriate reading)*

Choir: "Redeeming Love" *(Gaither Music Company)*

Speaker 2: I gather that one of the key words in that verse is "LOVE"?

Speaker 1: Correct. Our **Love** at Christmas is shown in various ways. We give baskets to needy people, we give to our favorite charities, or drop money in kettles, all very worthy causes. And it makes us feel very good inside. We feel our duty has been done for another year. But I have often wondered if the needy folks to whom the baskets are delivered know the reason why we are doing it.

Speaker 2: You mean, when the Lord has taken His place in our hearts, we cannot help but to radiate His **Love** to others?

Speaker 1: Precisely. It should be apparent from our walk of life that we belong to Christ. Does it move us to tears realizing that God **Loved** us so much that He sent His only Son to die for our sins? Do we perceive each person as someone "made in the image of God," who is in need of a Savior? Are we as excited as the shepherds were?

Narrator: "The shepherds returned, glorifying and praising God for all the things they had heard and seen, which were just as they had been told" (Luke 2:20, *New International Version*).

SOLO: "He Started the Whole World Singing" *(Gaither Music Company)*

SPEAKER 1: **Joy** was written all over the faces of the shepherds, for they had been witnesses to this great act of God. I like to think it must have been apparent to all who met them.

SPEAKER 2: Folks seem to smile more at Christmastime, and generally speaking, everyone seems to enjoy the season and all it brings. But I have to admit that **Joy** isn't always noticeable in my life. Circumstances and the situation I may find myself in on any given day, have much to do with the way I show forth **Joy**.

SPEAKER 1: But did you know that we are still able to experience the real **Joy** of Christmas, even though there would be no presents for us under the tree, nor any of the trimmings we associate with the season? Hard to believe, you say, yet it is true. Real **Joy** is not dependent on this world's goods, but it has to do with the state of our hearts. If Jesus lives in our hearts, there will be **Joy**—the kind that no one will be able to take away from us; nor can circumstances hinder it. Listen to what the prophet Habakkuk says about this.

NARRATOR: "Though the fig tree does not bud and there are no grapes on the vines, though the olive crop fails and the fields produce no food, though there are no sheep in the pen and no cattle in the stalls, yet I will rejoice in the Lord, I will be joyful in God my Savior" (Habakkuk 3:17, 18, *New International Version*).

CONGREGATION: "How Great Our Joy!" *(stanzas 1, 2, and 3)*

SPEAKER 2: I am beginning to learn more and more about being "ready for Christmas." Would you believe I never gave these things much thought? What about the **Peace** of Christmas? How would you define that?

SPEAKER 1: A **Peace** that we can have even when all things fall apart around us. A **Peace** in the midst of storms, diseases, financial disasters, family disagreements, strife, wars and rumors of war, and it will be an everlasting **Peace**. It comes from the Prince of Peace, Jesus Christ himself.

NARRATOR: "And he will be called Wonderful Counselor, Mighty God, Everlasting Father, Prince of Peace. Of the increase of his government and peace there will be no end" (Isaiah 9:6, 7, *New International Version*).

CONGREGATION: "I Heard the Bells on Christmas Day"

SPEAKER 2: From listening to you, I feel I missed out on much of the real meaning of Christmas. What must I do to be ready for Christmas, to have the Savior of the world come into my heart and house?

SPEAKER 1: That is something that only God can tell you. For, you see, He deals with each person in His own unique way. He prepares our hearts so that we are ready to receive the Christ. He points out the things that have to change in our lives, the sins we have to confess, and He keeps prompting us until we respond.

Take a closer look at the persons who are part of the Christmas story, how each one is made ready for this great event, and yet how they all are different. Some are prepared immediately, others have to go through a refining process. Take, for instance, Mary, the mother of our Lord. She says after the angel tells her what is going to happen: "I am the Lord's servant. May it be to me as you have said." Immediately she is prepared for this great event that is to take place.

TRIO: "Lo, How a Rose E'er Blooming" *(stanzas 1 and 2)*

SPEAKER 1: On the other hand, you have Zechariah, the father of John the Baptist, who is struck dumb after hearing the angel's message, because at that moment he is not prepared to accept the news. God gave him nine months to reflect on God's message and to get ready for Christ's birth.

Looking at the shepherds, you will find no hesitation on their part after they heard the angel's message; nor were they worried about their sheep, which were, after all, their livelihood. No, there is great willingness to go (actually they hurried) and see for themselves, "This thing that has happened, which the Lord has told us about" (Luke 2:15, *New International Version*).

CONGREGATION: "Ring the Bells" *(Singspiration Music)*

SPEAKER 1: Let's not forget the wise men. They followed a star, and that became a journey that took months, most likely. They were persistent, even when they met King Herod and got the royal runaround. They kept on searching and did not rest until they found Him, whose star they had followed from afar.

MEN'S TRIO: "We Three Kings of Orient Are"

SPEAKER 1: As you can see, each person reacted differently, yet each in his own way was being prepared. God is still preparing hearts. Maybe He is urging you tonight to accept Him as Lord and Savior and to celebrate Christmas as you have never celebrated it before.
   The sad thing is that not everyone wanted to be prepared for His coming so many years ago and some even now reject Him.

NARRATOR: "He came to that which was his own, but his own did not receive him" (John 1:11, *New International Version*).

SPEAKER 1: But He comes to those who choose to get prepared for His coming, whose hearts have been changed; whose lives reflect the **Love, Joy** and **Peace,** which they received from the Christ, and who are now carrying that message to others.
NARRATOR: "Yet to all who received him, to those who believed in his name, he gave the right to become children of God—children born not of natural descent, nor of human decision or a husband's will, but born of God" (John 1:12, 13, *New International Version*).
SPEAKER 2: Those of us who have received Him, what prevents us to bring praise and honor to Him who gave His all for us? Let's raise our voices in grateful song for God's unspeakable Gift and, like all the others before us, let's spread the message far and wide.

CONGREGATION: "O Holy Night!" *(stanza 1),* and "O Come, All Ye Faithful" *(chorus only, two times, once with organ, once without)*

This program may be followed by a short meditation. Contents of the message could be "no room in the inn." This may be followed with a candlelight service. "Silent Night! Holy Night!" may be sung during the service.

Ready for Christmas

Why Should I Be Thankful?

Lillian Robbins

Characters:
FRED (or FREEDA)
KATRINA, mother
TRISH, small girl, nonspeaking
MR. CRAMDON
MRS. CRAMDON
JACK
ANTONIA
LATONYA
STEPHANIE
MRS. LASSITER
HECTOR
BERNARD
MRS. FOSTER
LESLIE
NELLIE, young lady
WILLIE
ALICE
FOUR OTHER LITTLE CHILDREN, nonspeaking
SINGING GROUP

Setting: Outside in a park setting

Props: Park bench, stool, crutches, white-tipped stick, basket, clothes, food, garbage can, piece of sandwich, wheelchair, pencils, stroller, money, paper list.

Act I

Fred is seated on park bench.

FRED *(rubbing foot):* Oh, it hurts so bad. I wonder when it will ever get well. The doctor said it was just a sprained ankle, so why does it hurt so bad? I haven't been able to jog in three days. I'll get out of shape in no time. Oh, it hurts so bad!

If that kid hadn't left his roller blades on the sidewalk, I wouldn't have tripped and hurt my ankle. Misery, misery, nothing but misery these days. I don't know why people are making so much to-do about Thanksgiving. That's all I hear lately. I don't see where I've got anything to be thankful for.

KATRINA *(comes along carrying child on her hip):* Good afternoon, Sir.

FRED: Why in the world are you carrying a child that big? You ought to let her walk. Don't you know you'll ruin your back?

KATRINA *(happily):* I don't think so, Sir. You see, this burden is all carried with love. Trish can't walk, but she loves to come down to the park and watch the other children play. We come down here every day. We both enjoy our time together. God has truly blessed us. By the way, when we came up I noticed you were rubbing your foot. Is something wrong?

FRED *(grumpy):* There sure is. I fell because some kid left his roller blades on the sidewalk. That put a stop to most of my activities for a few days.

KATRINA: I'm sorry. I do hope your foot will feel better soon.

FRED: Yeah, me, too.

KATRINA: Good-bye now. *(Exits.)*

FRED: Hmm-m, that child can't walk. I wonder what makes her mother so happy.

WILLIE *(approaches, using crutches with difficulty):* Do you mind if I sit here by you for a minute?

FRED: It's a free country. Do whatever you want.

WILLIE: Thanks. These crutches really wear me out. I just can't seem to get the hang of it.

FRED: Why don't you just throw them away and try it without them?

WILLIE: Oh, I can't do that. The doctor is going to amputate my foot.

FRED: You mean—cut it off?

WILLIE: Yes, I'm going into the hospital right after Thanksgiving.

FRED: I guess you don't have much to be thankful for, do you?

WILLIE: Oh, no, that's not the way it is. I'm very thankful I have one good foot. I will still be able to get around after the surgery. It's just going to take a little getting used to. *(Slowly stands.)* I better be going. I'm rather slow moving about, and if the weatherman is right, rain is coming in. I don't want to get caught out in the rain. So long.

FRED: Yeah, so long. *(Willie exits.)* That would be kind of bad, having your foot cut off. But I don't understand how he can be so cheerful.

MRS. FOSTER (*Leslie and four other little children follow*): Come on, children. We have just two more blocks to go. The neighbor next door said there is a store down that way somewhere.

FRED: Excuse me, what kind of store are you looking for?

MRS. FOSTER: Some place I can buy school supplies. We've just moved here, and when the children went to school this morning, the teacher gave them a list of things they need.

FRED: You're going to the right place then. Sammy's Variety sells stuff like that.

MRS. FOSTER: I hope it's not an expensive store. Where we came from, the children didn't have to buy all these things.

FRED: The prices are better at Sammy's than at the mall.

MRS. FOSTER: Well, we better hurry along. Come on, children. (*They leave.*)

(*Hector and Mrs. Lassiter approach. She uses a white-tipped stick.*)

HECTOR: Mrs. Lassiter, we are almost at our spot now. Just a little farther along this path.

FRED: Where are you two going?

HECTOR: Just down to the water fountain. Mrs. Lassiter likes to sit there and listen to the water fall over the rocks. She can't see, but she enjoys what she can hear.

MRS. LASSITER: It gives me such a wonderful feeling. In my mind, I can see the mountain stream back home where I grew up. The water rippled over the rocks, and wild flowers grew along the banks. There was one area where the most beautiful violets you ever saw came back year after year.

FRED: You weren't blind then?

MRS. LASSITER: Oh, no, this just happened five years ago.

FRED: I guess you don't have much to be thankful for.

MRS. LASSITER: Of course I do. I have wonderful memories of things I saw before I lost my sight. I can almost see those big speckled trout jumping in the streams now. And I saw my grandchildren's lovely faces. They have grown since then, but I know how they look.

HECTOR: We better go on, Mrs. Lassiter. There are a few things I want to do for you before your children come for Thanksgiving.

MRS. LASSITER: And you know they will all be here for three days.

(Mrs. Lassiter and Hector leave. Latonya and Stephanie enter carrying a big basket of clothes and food.)

LATONYA: Stephanie, if it's getting too heavy, we can stop for a few minutes.

STEPHANIE: Let's do that. *(Puts basket down.)* I didn't think clothes would be this heavy. I guess it's all those cans of food we put in there.

LATONYA: Maybe we should have carried the clothes and then brought the food later.

STEPHANIE: But it's going to be Thanksgiving, and people are going to need extra food for Thanksgiving dinner.

FRED: Where are you girls going with that big basket?

LATONYA: To the church to take clothes and food.

FRED: Why do they need all that stuff?

STEPHANIE: Mister, don't you know there are a lot of people out of work? They don't have money to buy warm clothes, and sometimes they don't even have enough food to eat unless somebody helps them.

FRED: I reckon you're right. But why don't they get a job?

LATONYA: There are more people than there are jobs. God wants us to help each other. Come on, Stephanie. We can make it now. *(They leave.)*

(Jack enters and looks in garbage can, takes wrapper from a fast-food restaurant, finds piece of sandwich, puts to mouth to bite.)

FRED *(walks over to Jack):* What are you doing, Boy? Don't eat that garbage. It will make you sick.

JACK: Mister, you must not know what it's like to be hungry.

FRED: I've never been hungry enough to eat out of a garbage can.

JACK: What would you do if you didn't have any food or any money?

FRED: I don't know, but—wait a minute. Look right down that way. *(Points.)* There's a center where they have food. I think they help people in situations like yours. Go on down there and ask them to help you.

JACK *(big smile):* Thanks, Mister. *(Leaves.)*

FRED: Hmm-m. He said thanks. People don't ever say that to me. Of course I don't ever do anything for them to thank me for, I guess.

(Mrs. Cramdon enters, pushing Mr. Cramdon in a wheelchair.)

Why Should I Be Thankful?

Mr. Cramdon: Hello there, friend.

Fred: You must think I'm somebody else. I don't even know you.

Mr. Cramdon: I know that, but I like to think that everybody is my friend.

Fred: Oh, I didn't know what you meant.

Mrs. Cramdon: We're going down to the gardens. Mr. Cramdon loves to sit there and look at the beautiful beds of mums.

Mr. Cramdon: I just never can decide which is my favorite. Now you take those purple ones. They make me think of a king's palace. But then those spider mums—well, I don't really know what they are, but I call them spider mums because they have all those little petals; they are special. Of course, those little white ones that look like snowballs—

Mrs. Cramdon: We better go now, Dear. You could just stay right here and talk about flowers all day.

Mr. Cramdon *(speaking to Fred):* Good-bye, now.

Fred: Good-bye. *(The Cramdons leave.)*

Antonio *(carrying pencils):* Mister, will you buy a pencil from me?

Fred: Why should I buy a pencil?

Antonio: Everybody can use pencils. And I need the money.

Fred: Why do you need the money?

Antonio: It's getting a little too cold to walk around with these worn-out shoes on. I put paper in them to try to stop up the holes in the shoe soles, but that doesn't last too long.

Fred: Money for a pencil won't buy shoes. Shoes cost a lot of money.

Antonio: I know that. But when I sell enough pencils, I'll have enough money to buy shoes.

Fred: Well, just sell your pencils to someone else. I don't need them.

(Antonio leaves. Singing group comes by singing a happy song—your choice.)

Fred: Well, now, why are you kids going around singing at the top of your voices?

Alice: We like to sing happy songs because we are happy people.

Fred: What's to be so happy about?

Alice: We're all the best of friends. We like being with our friends, and we like to sing. Besides, you know it's almost Thanksgiving. *(Leave singing.)*

Fred: Thanksgiving. Some of these people I've seen today have all kinds of problems, but they seem to be happy anyway. I guess I've been missing something. I wonder—what can I do to find some of that happiness? Maybe I need to change my attitude. Well, I guess I'll just hobble on home now. *(Leaves.)*

Act II

Next day in the park, Fred is sitting on the bench. A big stroller, clothes and food are beside him.

FRED: I hope I'll see some of those same people I saw here yesterday. I thought about them half the night and finally decided what I could do.

KATRINA *(approaches):* Good afternoon, Sir. How is your foot today?

FRED: It's much better. I'm glad you came by again. I have something for you.

KATRINA: For me?

FRED: Yes, I thought about this stroller I had seen in the store, and I could tell it would be just right for your little girl. *(Pushes stroller toward her.)* Here, try it.

KATRINA *(puts Trish in stroller):* Oh, that's wonderful. She will really enjoy riding in this. Thank you, Sir. Thank you very much.

FRED: You're welcome, ma'am. Have a good time in the park.

(Katrina and Trish leave. Willie approaches with crutches.)

FRED *(calls out):* Hello, there. Won't you come over and have a seat?

WILLIE: Thanks. *(Sits down.)*

FRED: How are you getting along with those crutches today?

WILLIE: I think I can manage a little better. I made an adjustment here, *(Indicates handhold.)* and they seem easier to handle now.

FRED: When did you say you are going to the hospital?

WILLIE: The day after Thanksgiving.

FRED: By the way, *(Puts hand out for handshake.)* my name is Fred.

WILLIE: Hi, Fred, I'm Willie.

FRED: Which hospital will you go to?

WILLIE: County General.

FRED: Maybe I can get over to see you while you are laid up.

WILLIE: That will be good. I don't have many folks around here. *(Stands.)* I better be on my way now. See you.

FRED: I'll pray for you. See you, Willie.

Why Should I Be Thankful?

(Willie leaves. Nellie enters crying. She sits on a stool a distance away.)

FRED *(going over to her):* Why are you crying? Did you get hurt?

NELLIE *(looking up):* No. But I — I— I just miss my mom so much.

FRED: Where is your mom?

NELLIE: She lives across the country. When I got married and moved way out here, I didn't know I would miss her so much.

FRED: Where is your husband?

NELLIE: At work.

FRED: Why don't you go to see your mom?

NELLIE: It costs too much to fly home. If I could just talk to her, I would feel better. But we don't have a phone.

FRED: No phone? I thought everybody had a phone.

NELLIE: We will get one just as soon as we get some money ahead. *(Starts crying again.)* It's the first time I won't be home for Thanksgiving.

FRED: Wait a minute. I've got an idea. Look right over there, down the street. *(Points.)* There is a pay phone. You can call from there.

NELLIE: I don't have any money.

FRED *(takes money from pocket and gives it to her):* Here, this should be enough. Go on over there and call your mom.

NELLIE: Thanks, Mister. *(Leaves.)*

MRS. FOSTER *(enters, children follow, Leslie is crying):* Stop that crying, Leslie. I told you I am doing the best I can. I didn't have enough money yesterday, and I have only two dollars more today. That just won't buy everything on this list. Some things must be left off until next week.

(Bernard enters and sits quietly on stool at far side of stage.)

FRED *(going over to little girl, pats her on the head):* Why are crying, little girl?

MRS. FOSTER: She is disappointed because I can't get all of her supplies. I wish I could get everything, but I can't. I told her the teacher will just have to get somebody to share with her until I can do something about it.

FRED: How much money do you need?

MRS. FOSTER: About five dollars, I think. I hope my husband will have some extra money when he gets paid next week.

FRED *(takes money out of his pocket and gives it to her):* Maybe this can help. Then this cute little girl can stop crying.

MRS. FOSTER: Oh, thank you, Sir. Thank you very much.
LESLIE (*looks up and smiles*): Thanks, Mister.

(*They leave. Mrs. Lassiter and Hector enter.*)

FRED: Well, how is the lady from the mountains today?
MRS. LASSITER: Oh, just fine. God has created a beautiful day. I can
   feel the warm sunshine on my shoulders.
FRED: I see that you and your friend are going to the fountain again.
MRS. LASSITER: Sure. I just love to walk down there in the beautiful
   fall weather like this. Feels like it will be just right for Thanksgiving.
FRED: I hope so. And I hope all your family gets to see you.
MRS. LASSITER: Hector is a smart boy, and we have everything ready.
   It will be a happy Thanksgiving for us. (*She and Hector start to walk
   on. She turns back.*) Oh, and I hope you have a happy Thanksgiving
   too.
FRED: Thanks. Good-bye. Maybe I will see you again.

(*Mrs. Lassiter and Hector leave. Singing group can be heard in the distance.*)

FRED (*calls out*): Hey, kids, could you come over and sing for me?
ALICE (*enters with kids*): Sure. Come on, kids, let's sing a special song
   for the man. (*They sing a song of your choice. After song, Alice speaks
   again.*) Come on, everybody, we have to go now.
FRED: Have a happy Thanksgiving.
ALICE AND GROUP: You too. (*Leave.*)

(*Fred is sitting on bench again. Antonio walks by keeping his distance from
Fred.*)

FRED: Hey, Boy, come on over here.

(*Antonio comes near.*)

FRED: What's your name?
ANTONIO: Antonio.
FRED: Well, Antonio, you know what? I found out I need a whole
   bunch of pencils. Here is some money. (*Hands him bills.*) Let me
   buy all your pencils, and you can go on and get your shoes.

(*Antonio gives him the pencils and takes the money.*)

Why Should I Be Thankful?

ANTONIO: Oh, boy! Thanks! *(Runs off the stage.)*

(The Cramdons approach.)

FRED *(stands and shakes hands with Mr. Cramdon):* Good evening, Friend. You know, I never did learn your name.
MR. CRAMDON: I'm Albert Cramdon.
FRED: And I'm Fred. It's good to know you. How is it going today?
MR. CRAMDON: Wonderful. I think the flowers were as pretty yesterday as I have ever seen them. A whole bed of those little yellow cushion mums are just opening up.
FRED: You know, I might like to walk down there with you one day.
MR. CRAMDON: That would be great. How about now?
FRED: I still have a couple more things to do today, but one day soon for sure.
MRS. CRAMDON: He will like somebody else to talk to other than me. He's already told me his stories so many times.
FRED: We'll get together one day soon. Now you just enjoy those flowers today.
MR. CRAMDON: Sure will. Good-bye, Friend.
FRED: Good-bye to you, too, until we see each other again.

(The Cramdons leave. Fred sits down.)

BERNARD *(walks over to bench):* Do you mind if I sit here for a little while?
FRED: Sure, come on. Sit right here beside me. What's your name, Son?
BERNARD: Bernard. I've just moved here and I don't know anyone yet.
FRED: Well, my name is Fred, and now you know someone.
BERNARD: I really am looking for a friend. I've been sitting over there watching you and I think anybody as kind to people as you are would be a good friend.
FRED: You know something, Bernard? For a long time I didn't know how important friends were. But I'm learning about it now. I'd like to be your friend.
BERNARD: My mom is going to cook Thanksgiving dinner. Would you come over and eat with us?
FRED: Well, now that you mention it, I don't have any plans. Sure, I would love to come.

(Stephanie and Latonya enter carrying basket.)

Why Should I Be Thankful?

FRED: Wait a minute, girls. Looks like you are on your way to the church.

LATONYA: You're right. We picked up some more clothes from some of our neighbors. Even got coats this time.

FRED: I was hoping you would come by. I've got something too, and I thought maybe you could tell me who to talk to down there.

STEPHANIE: We see Mr. Dozier.

FRED: Do you mind if I go along with you now?

STEPHANIE: That will be great. It will help make a lot more people happy on Thanksgiving.

FRED: Come on, Bernard. We may as well meet some more friends. By the way girls, what are your names?

STEPHANIE: Stephanie.

LATONYA: Latonya.

FRED: I'm Fred, and this is Bernard. He is new in town. *(Fred picks up clothes and all start to leave.)* Bernard, I think both of us have found new friends, and I'll bet there are a lot more around here. You know, I think it really will be a happy Thanksgiving this year. We certainly have a lot to thank God for. Let's all sing that song—let's see, how does it go? "Come, ye thankful people come."

(Bernard and girls join in and they sing as they leave. Another appropriate song may be used.)

Why Should I Be Thankful?